No More Secrets

Healing from Domestic Violence

No More Secrets

Healing from Domestic Violence

*By a sisterhood of survivors: Allison, Becca, Cecilia,
Donna-Marie, Olive, and Selma*

Facilitated by Carole Thompson and Sherry Katz

Edited by Sharon Johnson

ISBN: 978-1-945446-06-1

LEON SMITH
PUBLISHING

www.LeonSmithPublishing.com

Praise for No More Secrets

"Domestic violence is not an issue that belongs to any one socioeconomic group, race, neighborhood, or cultural group. As long as it is happening to any one individual or family in our community, it is an issue we all need to consider ourselves accountable for. I thank the women who contributed to *No More Secrets* for doing the hard work of turning their painful experiences into a powerful resource, not only for survivors, but for informing, empowering, and inspiring the entire community to act. The work is a testament to the strength of these survivors as well as the incredible work being done by The Second Step. Newton is fortunate to have The Second Step and its strong network of survivors as partners in our efforts to eradicate domestic violence."

— Mayor Setti Warren, Newton, Massachusetts

" 'You may be feeling scared and isolated, with nowhere to turn. But we are here to tell you that you are not alone.' So begins this powerful book, written by six survivors of intimate partner violence, all of whom participated in the Narrative Healing Group at The Second Step, a domestic violence organization located outside of Boston.

These brave women come from a wide variety of backgrounds, yet they found each other through the group and formed a sisterhood, supporting each other as they shared stories of trauma, coping, and resilience. In this book, they pay it forward to others who might be struggling with the same issues. What is remarkable about these women is not that they found each other and built a community of mutual belonging; that's just what happens when women come together to share common experiences. No, what is remarkable is that they decided to share their experiences with others — and oh so creatively!

Through vivid vignettes, these authors describe their journeys from sometimes painfully difficult childhoods to their first encounters with romance and love, then through trauma and isolation to recovery, and finally, to thriving. Interspersed with these powerful accounts are pieces of advice to other women, descriptions of the inner workings of the Narrative Healing Group, and theories to frame their stories.

It is impossible not to come away feeling moved and inspired. Readers who themselves have endured intimate partner violence will find many pieces of hard-won wisdom in these pages. Indeed, we will all feel less alone thanks to the courage and perseverance of these six women."

— Lisa Goodman, PhD, Professor, Department of Counseling and Developmental Psychology, Lynch School of Education, Boston College and Co-Author of *Listening to Battered Women: A Survivor-Centered Approach to Advocacy, Mental Health, and Justice*

Table Of Contents

PART I
Get Real: Acknowledging What's True

PART II
Get Help: Finding The Strength To Reach Out

PART III
Get Healed: Moving From Surviving To Thriving

Dedication From The Group

Dear Wife, Sister, Mother, Daughter, Friend:

You may be feeling scared and isolated, with nowhere to turn. But we are here to tell you that you are not alone. You have us. We are a small group of women who have been right where you are and know exactly what you are going through.

We wrote this book to tell you that domestic violence does not need to define you, nor does it need to shape your or your children's future. There is the possibility of a rich, fulfilling life after domestic violence. It is yours for the taking. Our hope is that this book will help guide you there.

Domestic violence comes in many forms, and each of our stories is different. But we have much in common and much we can learn from our shared experiences.

The very fact that you're holding this book in your hands shows what women just like you are capable of. Take a step. Turn the page. Things will get better from here.

Dedication To Our Children

To my daughter, Kayla, the reason why I don't give up. My hope for you is that you know you are valued and cherished more than words can ever express. Your story is yet to be written, and may the words contained always be yours. Always smile!

— Love, Becca

This book is dedicated to my daughter, Kiara, whom I love very much. Thank you for loving me and making me smile.

— Love, Donna-Marie

To Alyssia, Kaleb, and Joshua: My hope for your future is for you to know that you are marvelous individuals. I pray that you continue to encourage, lift up, and inspire everyone around you. I pray that self-doubt is your enemy, as self-doubt stopped me from reaching my potential in life. I pray that you don't dream of a better life but instead hold a vision of the greatest life lived. Think of it this way: A dream you can awaken from; a vision you can bring into fruition.

— Love, Allison

To my children: I wish you well as you journey through life. With every milestone that you meet, I hope it's as smooth as it can be. My children, "I" is what you make of it. My wish for you is that you embrace your life with great enthusiasm. Life can be challenging. As you grow, I hope you can acknowledge every hurdle as a chance to grow, as a lesson well learned. My wish for you is that you embrace your passions, that you are truthful about who you are. Let no one change your destiny. I love you all.

— Love, Olive

Thank you, God, for blessing me with my wonderful kids, and thank you, my children, for the love and support you've given me. We hold tight together—we hold hands together and try to reach one another. I want you to find love and happiness in life. Finish school, so that you will have happy lives and work that you love. Focus—there are so many distractions in life, but if you focus, you will get there. There will be a lot of bumps in the road, but, once you get there, you will see all of your accomplishments, all you've done.

— Love, Cecilia

I would like to dedicate this book to my three beautiful children and three amazing grandchildren that give me the strength and will to keep going. Mike, Kristie, and Isaiah—you are my world! Samantha, Kendra, and Hunter—my little loves. Thank you for giving me a reason to go on, without *all* of you I don't know what I would have done. To my youngest (the product of my relationship mentioned in this book), always remember how special you are. I would never change you for the world. I was so blessed the day you came into my life!

— Love, Selma

Dedication From Carole Thompson Director Of Community Programs At The Second Step

To the *No More Secrets* sisterhood:

My relationship with each of you humbles me . . . through the years and the tears, the laughter and the lessons learned, through the triumphs and the disappointments . . . You are my most profound teachers.

I am honored that you have invited me to sit witness to your bonding, to your . . . to our . . . growing together.

From isolation, you came together . . . hesitantly. Little icebergs drifting together on this sea of unknowing . . . never touching, then sometimes even drifting away until the next time. Slowly, the ice began to melt, and, in this melting, your sisterhood began to sparkle, and the richness of your togetherness began to glow.

As you began to teach each other and grow together, each of you ultimately found your own strength, your own voice . . . the synergy of your bond encouraged the rising of your truest selves. For this is the gift you give to yourselves and to each other . . . the embracing of your authenticity, the celebration of the wonder of who you truly are.

I have been forever changed by the very act of sitting witness to your stories of strength, survival, and courage. I have witnessed the depth of your intense love for your children and the suffering you are willing to endure for their safety. I have witnessed your vulnerability and incredible strength. I have come to know your beautiful, loving, giving, creative, poetic selves.

I cherish the gift of your trust and the lessons you have taught me about love and life. You are my heroines. Thank you for including me in this precious circle.

Dedication From Sherry Katz
Second Step Volunteer And Co-Facilitator

To the amazing women of the Narrative Healing group:

It is an honor to bear witness to what you have endured, to laugh with you, and to learn from you. I am in awe of your resilience. You have faced pain and suffering and are now moving forward with courage and dignity—always loving and fiercely protecting your children and now learning to love yourselves.

Your writing of this book has been an act of affirmation and generosity. I have watched you support one another, adding insight, giving advice, using humor, but mostly truly listening and understanding, sharing your secrets and realizing that there's no shame in what happened to you; rather, that you are the heroines of your stories. And you have focused not only on one another, but also on how you can help others who might read this book—those who are experiencing abuse and those who are helplessly watching people they love being abused.

One of you once said that you believed in angels on earth, helping us each find our way. I believe you are each other's angels.

> The Department of Justice defines domestic violence as "a pattern of abusive behavior in any relationship that is used by one partner to gain or maintain power and control over another intimate partner." Domestic violence can be physical, psychological, sexual, or economic actions or threats, including behaviors that "intimidate, manipulate, humiliate, isolate, frighten, terrorize, coerce, threaten, blame, hurt, injure, or wound someone." Relationships involving domestic violence may differ in terms of the severity, but the primary goal is control.

In this book, you will meet survivors of domestic violence. While they are of different ages, circumstances, and ethnic backgrounds, they share the experience of Intimate Partner Violence and the ensuing trauma and isolation that is a trademark of this dynamic. Their stories powerfully illustrate the importance of long-term, supportive relationships for true healing to occur. Recovering from the traumatic dynamic of Intimate Partner Violence is complicated, because the impact of trauma is profound. Like cancer, trauma can never be completely "cured;" it can only be treated in an effort to put it into remission.

One misconception held by many well-intentioned people is that breaking away from an abusive relationship is simply a choice. We wonder: "Why doesn't she just leave?" We assume that there are systems in place to protect victims and hold perpetrators accountable. Unfortunately, it is not that simple. A grave error in this way of thinking is failing to realize that the very act of survivors taking control and leaving actually makes the situation more dangerous.

Fear of being injured or killed keeps many women in abusive relationships, and their concerns are legitimate. In her groundbreaking book, *The Power to Break Free*, Anisha Durve asserts that the risk of death or injury to a victim is greatest when leaving an abusive relationship or shortly thereafter. Nearly 75% of battered women seeking emergency medical services sustained injuries after leaving their abuser. According to the National Network to End Domestic Violence, on average, three women die at the hands of a current or former intimate partner every day.

Another misconception is that once an individual survivor deals with the immediate crisis, the problem has been solved. That is definitely not the case.

Escaping the dangerous situation is only the beginning. The impact of trauma, the isolation from supportive relationships, and the shame are all so debilitating. The loss of self-esteem erodes the ability to trust one's own instincts. Survivors need support and community for every step in their process of healing.

Dr. Judith Herman, Associate Clinical Professor of Psychiatry at Harvard Medical School and Director of Training at the Victims of Violence Program at Cambridge Hospital, is a national expert in the field of trauma and domestic violence. In her landmark book, *Trauma and Recovery,* Dr. Herman notes that traumatic events such as domestic violence destroy one's "fundamental assumptions about safety in the world (and) the positive value of the self."

She identified three stages through which trauma survivors must pass in order to successfully recover:

1. Establishing safety

2. Remembering, mourning, and reconstructing the trauma story

3. Restoring the connection between survivors and their community

Dr. Herman also found that, in the final stage of healing, many survivors seek to make something meaningful out of their abuse, by sharing their stories and lessons learned. By having the opportunity to "pay it forward," they heal themselves in the process.

The Second Step programs, designed with these three stages in mind, seek to foster long-term relationships with, and among, survivors of domestic violence. It is our commitment to partner with survivors, wherever they are on that spectrum of enduring or healing from abuse, that distinguishes our work.

The first critical step is to secure safety, a process that can present multiple, shifting challenges. The subsequent steps to recovery vary from person to person because recovering from trauma involves an individual's ability to re-establish trust in a world where it has been shattered, to find healthy ways of coping with the symptoms caused by the abuse, and to weave a web of connections that make it possible for a person to reclaim herself and her life.

Because one of the most devastating side effects of domestic violence is isolation, we strive to build a healing community of non-judgmental, relational support. We believe that a healthy network of support is essential to a survivor's ability to stabilize and stay safe over time. In our IMAGINE Program (an acronym that stands for Inspiration, Motivation, And Growth In Networks that Empower), we offer survivors opportunities to create connections among themselves and within the greater community. We believe in the power of sitting witness to survivors' incredible stories, of creating trusting relationships in an atmosphere of respect and non-judgment. And, even on the darkest days, we "hold the hope" for what is possible going forward.

This book is a product of the Narrative Healing group, one of several relational healing groups within the IMAGINE Program at The Second Step.

This book is also a love story. It is the story of a group of women who came together week after week to use their experiences to help educate others who are stuck in the devastating reality of Intimate Partner Violence and who were forever changed in the process. Their intention to help others is consistent with that final stage of healing from abuse. What they didn't anticipate was just how powerful their sisterhood would become and the impact that this experience would have on their lives. As they sat together and witnessed each other's stories of pain and triumph, as they told their "shameful secrets," they began to change and heal in the safety of this precious circle. They've held each other, they've challenged each other, they've encouraged each other to be true to themselves, and in so doing they have discovered the profound healing power of connection.

This book is more than a "feel good" endeavor. A series of studies, first published in the *Journal of Personality and Social Psychology,* supports this type of work. Social psychologist Gregory Walton designed what he termed a "belonging intervention" to help people who are going through a tough time. He describes this type of intervention as storytelling, a way for participants to take their traumatic experiences and contain them, to put them in a box, as Walton says, with "a beginning, a middle, and an end." As a consequence, the meaning of the negative experience is constrained, and people understand that when bad things happen it's not just them, they are not alone, and that it's something that passes. Perhaps even better, telling their stories gave the women an opportunity to rewrite them, adding their own hopeful ending.

"Just like the lotus, we too have the ability to rise from the mud, bloom out of the darkness, and radiate into the world."
— Author unknown

PART I

GET REAL:
Acknowledging What's True

Whispers from A Sister

Listen to your gut.

**If something doesn't feel right, it probably isn't.
Trust the gift of your own intuition.**

STOP BELIEVING THE LIES.

HEAR YOUR VOICE INSTEAD OF THE VOICE OF YOUR ABUSER.

YOU are not responsible.   Listen to your INNER VOICE.

**It is the master technique of the abuser
to get you to believe that you're the
one that's responsible.
Come on, already. Just how many "walls" do you
think people will believe you can run into?**

Honey, there isn't enough concealer in the world.

Don't lie about why you're on crutches.

It would be easier if there were a bruise on the outside,
rather than on the inside.

Cut the bullshit. You don't have to lie for him.

If something makes you feel uncomfortable, don't
deny it.

The Women Of The Second Step Narrative Healing Group

That summer, I was officially homeless, and it was the first time I had to rely on an abusive man. Sleeping in his garage, in tents, and in shelters, I endured five years of homelessness.

— Becca

When I had the chance to play, I was very happy, running free, climbing my grandmother's apple and plum trees.

— Cecelia

After the divorce I went off to Boston to find myself and instead found my abuser.

— Selma

I didn't fit in anywhere — home, school, community — none of my three worlds.

— Donna-Marie

I was a quiet, mild, and giving person. I had a personality that he preyed on.

— Olive

At the age of twenty-six, after a particularly abusive relationship, I decided I wanted a better life.

— Allison

At the first meeting of the Narrative Healing Book Group, Carole Thompson, The Second Step Director of Community Programs, tacks a few oversized sheets of paper to the wall and stands at the ready, thick blue marker in hand, as the women of the group begin to craft some ground rules. No one holds back, and the words come faster than Carole can write:

- Respect each other. What is said in this room stays in this room.

- Resist making broad, sweeping statements that aren't true.

- Hold each other accountable. If we are speaking bullshit, or saying something not true to ourselves, call each other on it.

- Respect everyone's "air time." Make sure everyone has the opportunity to speak.

- Don't interrupt.

- Be honest.

- Don't judge. We all are or have been victims and don't need to be victimized again.

- Help, encourage, and validate each other.

- Respect that we each have our own truth.

- Notice who *isn't* speaking, and try to draw her out.

- Respect each person's right *not* to speak.

- When there's a conflict in the group, agree to resolve it as a group.

- Make a commitment to the group. Show up, even if you're in a bad place.

This is the first official meeting of the Narrative Healing Group. There's excitement, certainly, but also some nervous jitters. Not all of the women know each other, and it can be difficult to share intimate secrets, some of which have never been voiced before, with strangers. While that awkwardness among the group members will soon abate, for tonight it's decided that the women will first share a bit about their lives by writing about the circumstances that have brought them to this table. Here, in their own voices, is how each woman described herself to the circle that first night.

Becca: I was born in Boston. My mom was one of nine kids and was the only single parent of all her siblings. She was considered the black sheep of the family. I now know that she had borderline personality disorder. Her siblings did not treat her, or us kids, well.

One of my earliest memories is of sitting in a high chair. I couldn't have been much older than two. My father, her live-in boyfriend, threw spaghetti at us, and my mom scooped me up, and we left and moved to my grandparents' house. My mom had no freedom there and no goals for herself other than caring for us.

We were treated differently because we were considered "Welfarian" and not like the rest of the family. I had been brainwashed to hate my mother. "She is vermin. She is white trash," is what I heard over and over. My grandparents thought my mom was incompetent, and wanted to protect us from her. They were well meaning, but very flawed and abusive. My grandmother was an alcoholic, and my grandfather a workaholic. He used to chase me with a hot frying pan.

I quickly learned how not to piss them off.

They used to say I'd never amount to anything. They used to say I wasn't worth the spit out of my mother's mouth.

They abused my brother more, but encouraged him more also. He was a boy and considered more valuable.

We went to Boston public schools, and my mother, brother, and I moved into the housing projects when I was nine. My mom reveled in her freedom there and celebrated it with a revolving door of abusive men.

When my mom got pregnant again, my grandparents pulled us out of the projects and made us move back in with them. They enrolled us in Catholic School. I didn't even know how to recite the Hail Mary. The teachers thought I was Jewish.

When my grandmother had a heart attack, we moved yet again. This time we went to live with my aunt. I was in 9th grade and had to share a room with my 8th-grade brother. I had to maintain an A average and pay rent. When I got a C+ in math, I was grounded for the entire summer and was not allowed to eat at the table with the family.

One day my brother walked into the house and forgot to remove his shoes. My aunt flipped out. In hindsight, I realize she also must have had mental health issues. She went into a rage, ripped my posters off the bedroom walls, and then threw all of our stuff into garbage bags and drove us to my mother's house. She left us on the porch and drove away. This turned out to be the first of many of what I refer to as "garbage bag incidents."

Being back with my mother felt like *The Twilight Zone*. I had been brainwashed to hate her. Everything felt dirty to me. I couldn't understand why they put me back with her. Did they think I was like her?

I went on a hunger strike, which got me moved to another aunt's house in a nicer neighborhood. They put me downstairs with a futon in the basement. Despite having to work three jobs just so I could pay her rent, I managed to finish 11th in my class at the local Catholic high school. I was accepted to an all women's Catholic college.

I was the first in my family to go to college. Uncharacteristically, my family threw a big party for me. The party didn't last. While I "aced" the first semester at school, the second semester my aunt informed me that I couldn't return to her house when school finished because I had turned 18 and wasn't their responsibility anymore. At the end of the semester, my brother came in his car (a gift he had received from our family) to help me pack up and store my stuff until I could find a home.

That summer, I was officially homeless, and it was the first time I had to rely on an abusive man. Sleeping in his garage, in tents, and in shelters, I endured five years of homelessness.

Cecilia: I was born in a small village in Mexico, with only 15-20 houses, where we all knew each other. I came to the United States when I was 13 years old.

I am the second oldest of eight children, and all I remember of my mom is that she was angry and bitter, always yelling at me. I felt so ugly and so unwanted. Before I was born, my mom had lost a baby. She always talked about that beautiful white little baby and would say, "And then I had you, you ugly little Indian. I do not know why I didn't kill you when you were a baby."

All my life, I wanted her to touch me, to hug me, to touch my hair. I wanted her to acknowledge that I was there—that I was alive. I was more like a plant or a cat in the house. I wanted her to show her love. And she never did. She never showed any emotions—nothing. She was like metal—like she had no feelings. My sisters and brother and I never saw her teeth—she never smiled. She never seemed happy.

I never really understood. I knew I was different. But now I understand. I recently learned that my mom was forced to marry a man she didn't love. My grandmother forced her to marry him because his family had more money. My grandmother told her that by marrying him she would have enough food for her kids and would not suffer. His family also gave land to my mother's family as part of the arrangement. It's so sad. There was no love.

When I had the chance to play, I was very happy, running free, climbing my grandmother's apple and plum trees. My mother's house had many different types of flowers: roses, dahlias, and a lot of wildflowers. We'd cut the flowers and make pretend houses out of them. But most of the time, I had to help with my siblings.

My mother and father often fought. He would beat her up and I could see the red, purple, and pink marks on her back and arms. My grandmother would put hot water with salt and cream on the bruises to make the swelling go away.

My father would disappear for a week or two. I was always scared when he came home because I knew there would be a big fight. He would ask for food, and my mother would hide it and say we didn't have any. I would save my food and offer it to my father. He would refuse, saying, "No, you eat it." He was a good man when he was not drunk.

My mother's brother was a high school teacher and we were all supposed to respect him, but we heard people talking and accusing him of raping a girl. I was scared of him because he once touched my little breast and joked, "She don't have any." My mom just laughed.

My little sister was scared of him, too. We made fun and teased her, telling her, "He is going to get you." She would cry and curl up in a fetal position and tremble with fear. We thought it was funny. I was so sorry to find out later that he had raped her. I truly believe that my mom knew, because one night when my sister was sleeping I saw her checking her underpants. She got mad when she saw me watching and told me to go back to sleep.

I couldn't wait to get out of that place. I would see airplanes in the sky, and I had a feeling that one day I would fly. That was always my dream.

I had just finished 6th grade, and I had no idea that my life was about to change. My grandmother convinced my mother that I was old enough to get a job. I had to leave. She said she was going to get me a job as a nanny. She took my childhood; she took everything. A professor from a prestigious university used to visit my village every year. He knew my family and one day asked if I could come to the U.S. to help his wife care for their 3-year-old and 3-month-old children. In exchange, he promised to send me to school and send money back to my family. He promised to pay my family 500 pesos every month (the equivalent of 50 U.S. dollars). That wasn't anything to him, but it was a lot of money for my family.

I felt very sad because I would have to leave my brothers, and I was very scared. But part of me was also happy. I felt so important. I would be providing money for my family. My grandmother, mother, and aunt all went with me to Mexico City to meet the man and his family. I had never been on a train before. I'd never even seen a train. It looked like a giant snake to me. When we arrived in Mexico City, I couldn't believe what I saw. There were so many great big buildings, all of them made of glass from the ground all the way up to the sky. People were rushing everywhere, everything was moving, even the stairs, big and tall that went up forever! It was like magic. When I walked up to the doors of the embassy where we were to meet the man, the big glass doors just opened. I didn't touch anything, and they just opened! What would they do next? I thought the doors were going to suck me in! Nobody explained anything to me. I was so scared.

My job was to take care of the children. I did the laundry, cooking, dishes, and cleaning. The older boy liked me and wanted me to play with him all the time. We watched TV, played with his toys, or went to the park. I really liked my job. I felt special. The mom was nice to me, but the man of the house was always yelling. He was very powerful. He once told me that, if somebody wronged him, he would pay to have him killed. He made me feel uncomfortable; he would comment on my hair, my eyes. He would come out in a small towel after a shower. The lady of the house kept me close. I was never alone with him.

He let me talk to my parents only twice, and each time I had to pay for the phone call. My mother tried many times to send a letter or call me, but he wouldn't let her talk to me. And he never sent money to my family like he promised. He told me, "We cannot send any money to your mom, because you first have to pay for the cost of your plane ticket and all the paperwork we've had to do for you. It will take all the time you are here to pay us back."

I worked for that family as a nanny until I was 18. They never allowed me to go to school. They didn't teach me English. They said that when the little boy learned, he would teach me. I know now that I was like a slave. Now I know it was wrong, but then I didn't realize it. They did allow me to attend church, and that was how I was eventually able to get out of that situation and start to attend school. Unfortunately, that was also when I met my abuser.

> Cecelia is describing her experience as a victim of human trafficking. The National Institute of Justice defines human trafficking as "the recruitment, transport, transfer, harboring, or receipt of a person by such means as threat or use of force or other forms of coercion, of abduction, of fraud or deception for the purpose of exploitation." There are numerous reports of trafficking in the United States. In 2015 alone, the National Human Trafficking Resource Center received more than 21,000 calls from across the country, according to the U.S. Department of State "Trafficking In Persons Report."

I lost touch with my family and only spoke with my mom one or two times in 25 years. They thought I was dead. For many years, I would have dreams where I would see my father and rush to reach him, but he would vanish. Or I would dream of coming home but just couldn't get to the door of the house. I felt lost and so alone. I didn't know how to come back.

When I finally did get home, so much had changed. I didn't recognize anybody or anything. My family had rebuilt the house. It didn't look the same. There were no flowers anymore.

Selma: I was born in the mid-1960s to a woman of Mexican descent and a man of Irish/French heritage. I was the first grandchild in a large loving family. We were a Roman Catholic family who attended church, enjoyed family dinners, vacations, hiking, and camping. I was brought up in a beautiful family home in the suburbs of Western Massachusetts. It had natural woodwork and a total of 23 rooms. We were considered upper middle class in our prominent, Caucasian community. I spent my childhood embraced by grandparents, aunts, and uncles. I have fond childhood memories of love, guidance, learning, and security. I never went without. I could not have written a more beautiful childhood if I drafted it myself.

I attended Miss Jones School of Etiquette at age three to learn proper manners. I was a well-behaved girl. TV was not really part of my upbringing. I read a lot and was always encouraged to stimulate my mind. My father introduced me to numerous things in life: the planets, animals, history. The one hour of TV we were allowed each week consisted of Masterpiece Theater.

I inherited my mother's passion for the arts—dance and poetry in particular. She was a beautiful woman inside and out. God rest her soul! My father, though not a very emotional soul, enriched me. He taught me to be tough and how to survive. He educated me on the world, the arts, and would spend endless time camping, hiking, and traveling with me. He managed to be an outstanding father on top of working full time and attending college to obtain two masters degrees.

My grandfather was retired from the Army. He would spend time with me laughing and telling me stories. My grandmother taught me to cook. I loved the nights we would bake together, garden, all types of great things. I loved my "memiere." She would bring me to all of my doctor appointments because my mother couldn't bear to watch me get my shots. Afterward, we would go out for ice cream.

My grandmother was a phenomenal role model, but my mother was stifled and resentful. When she became pregnant with me she had to give up the dance contract she had with a modern dance company. She was a beautiful dancer, and I think she always resented that, through me, she lost her dreams. She was suppressed and very rigid with me growing up. My grandmother used to chastise her, saying, "You don't give the baby a bath when she's sleeping just because it's 5:00." They had a lot of power struggles. I have a better understanding now of her journey and where she came from.

One of my aunts would bring me to gymnastics, and, when she went off to college, I loved going to visit her and spending the night in her dorm. My uncles watched out for me and kept me safe. I would go running with one of them and the other would take me trick-or-treating on Halloween. My little sister was like my little doll. I was always playing with her even though I must admit at times she did get irritating. I loved her regardless! She turned out to be an amazing woman and mother and I am so happy and proud of her.

I was turning into a beautiful young woman, caring, hard-working, and loving. I played sports and had many friends. We would go skiing together and shopping at the mall. I did have boys that liked me, but I really didn't date through high school. I was more focused on my future. I graduated high school fifth in my class and full of life .

My family had big dreams for me. I was a straight-A student. They always felt I would be the first doctor in the family. I was considered the smart one. (Don't tell my sister.) Other family members had wonderful careers. I really cannot think of anyone in my family that wasn't well educated.

I decided to marry at age 18. My husband was a wonderful man. He was nine years older than me. I married him because he was in the Coast Guard, and I thought we would travel. I was young, but it was not uncommon to marry early during this period of time. But it turned out our marriage wasn't really a marriage. I felt like I was missing something. We were more business partners than anything. We built a wonderful business together, but the marriage didn't last. We had two beautiful children together that I love with all my heart and soul. He and I remain friends to this day. After the divorce I went off to Boston to find myself and instead found my abuser.

> **Selma's experience is contrary to typical stereotypes of victims of domestic violence. In fact, while the stereotypes may represent some dimensions of vulnerability, Intimate Partner Violence affects people from all socio-economic groups and educational, cultural, and religious backgrounds.**

Donna-Marie: I was born to a mom who was too young to care for me, so she gave me up for adoption. I was adopted by a family that already had their own children—all five of them boys. I would be the first girl. I don't think anyone took into account my race. My father's race was unclear—probably Portuguese, and my mother was white. My adopted family was black, and by all accounts I was raised as a black child. I don't think I really knew that there was a difference. I just thought I was a light-skinned black child. Growing up in the ghetto and being so light, I got teased about my color.

For the first six or seven years of my life, I don't remember anything—it was probably pretty good. I only think that because there was a picture of me at one of my birthday parties, and I was smiling and having fun. There was a picture of ME having FUN. I still have the picture.

For me, being a child, I felt unwanted. I didn't feel the security everyone must feel. I remember my mother telling me I was adopted, and the look on her face—the relief that she didn't give birth to me, like I wasn't really hers.

After she told me, I guess that was when my whole world changed. I became angry, distant, mean. I just wanted to fight the world. I wanted to belong, but I didn't know where I fit in. I didn't fit in at school, because I came from Boston and got bused to the suburbs. I didn't fit into my own community, because I was bused out of it every day for school. I didn't fit in anywhere—home, school, community—none of my three worlds.

I stayed like that—it seems like forever. I got into trouble a lot. I'd act up in school, get a beating at home. No matter what I did or didn't do, I wasn't believed. If someone blamed me for something I didn't do, they still thought I did it—it didn't matter. I guess that's when I learned to not have a voice. It's also where I learned that love hurts.

I found some things that I liked to do in life, like playing basketball. I learned that when I stepped onto the court I could focus only on basketball, and my troubles went away. They didn't seem to matter at all.

The fact that I went to church helped, and believing in God and believing that nothing in life happens without meaning or reason.

I had some really good people at church and school who influenced me and showed me that there was more to me than meets the eye. It was that little ray of hope that kept me going.

I wasn't even expected to graduate middle school; I was just taking up space. But once I got to high school, I realized that the only way to get out of my situation was to go to college. I went to a Christian college in the Berkshires. I remember going to college and going everywhere. I didn't come home except for Christmas. It didn't matter whose house I went to, I was welcomed. Half the time, my family never even knew where I was. Every time someone went home, I was in the car with her.

I didn't discover anything about my role as a leader until college. I became a leader. I was the captain of the basketball team. I was the class treasurer and then went on to be the class vice president. I thrived and felt like I finally had a purpose. I finally started to find my voice.

When I finished school and returned home, I lost all my support. I lost a lot, going back home. I didn't know if I was coming or going.

Olive: I was born on an island in the Caribbean and had a happy childhood there. I was the youngest of five children and always felt very protected and safe.

I lived with my mother and father and siblings. My mother started leaving the family to go and work in Boston when I was just five years old. She worked as a nanny and would be gone for five and six months at a time. My mom had a mission to pay off the mortgage on our house. During the time she was gone, my grandparents took on the parenting role. Some nights we would sleep at our parents' house, other times at our grandparents' house.

My grandmother was a strong force in my family. In fact, all of the women of my grandmother and mother's generation were sweet and kind but also awful—they were really feisty. They had a way with words. No one messed with them. They kept to themselves and were totally self-sufficient. They farmed fruit on their land and farmed and exported cotton. My grandmother owned a grocery store. My extended family of grandparents, great aunts, aunts, and cousins all had houses together with a shared yard.

My grandfather was a fisherman. I was closest to him. He *loved* me. He was always so happy to see me. He would take me to the store and buy me special things and tell me not to tell anyone else. He would bring me treats that he knew I loved. My grandmother would give each child $1.25 for bus money for the week. Sometimes my grandfather would call me aside and slip me another $20. I felt so safe with him. We had a real connection.

I did well in school and imagined I'd be a caretaker of some sort—either a doctor or a nurse. When I was 18, I came to Boston to visit my mother and sister. The plan was that I would then return home to complete my A Levels (the equivalent of 1st year college-level work). But I didn't realize that I was already pregnant. Once I did, I knew I couldn't go back to school—being pregnant was not allowed in our school. Instead, I stayed in Boston, and my mother and sister took care of me. I had my baby and took care of her and my sister's child while my mother and sister worked and took care of me. I wasn't street smart, so they would call from work to give me instructions.

When my daughter was two years old I got my first job as a nanny, but it turned out to be too far from home, so after several months I found another nanny job, closer to where I lived. In that time, our neighborhood had become dangerous. Someone was actually killed right on our doorstep. By then we realized that there was really no need for all of us to live together, and we all went in different directions.

Parenting and working were my life. I knew other nannies I would hang out with in the park, but I was very serious about working and parenting. My mother would take my daughter back home to the Caribbean for months at a time. During those times, I would focus on my work.

I met my abuser when I was twenty-five. I was a quiet, mild, and giving person. I had a personality that he preyed on. All the years that I was abused, I kept it from my family.

> In *The Power to Break Free,* author Anisha Durve lists common personality traits that make people more susceptible to this dynamic. These include:
>
> - Being a traditionalist — Believing in family values and female stereotypes
> - Being idealistic — Viewing marriage as an ideal to be attained and to strive for
> - Being vulnerable — Marked by being at a place of transition or uncertainty in life
> - Having a compassionate nature — Kind, patient, nurturing, loving
> - Feeling inferior — May admire and look up to spouse's position, wealth, or education and feel dependent on him for reassurance and support

Since leaving my abuser, I've grown so strong. Even though I'm the youngest in my family, they now treat me as the oldest child. They want my opinion on everything. They've watched my growth process and have told me they're so proud of me. I've stepped into the role of leader of the pack.

Allison: I was born in the small town of Winter Garden, Florida. At the age of eight I moved to Orlando, ten miles away. I was from a two-parent home. My mom was extremely strict raising us, but I now understand why. Overall, my relationship with my mom was great. Our relationship went through some difficult times when I was a young adult, but now I understand that she was trying to protect me from the world. She was the person who taught me all of my life lessons. She raised her children in alignment with the Bible, and the values and beliefs she instilled in me created the person you see today.

My mother was authoritarian. I guess another way to put it is, she yelled a lot. She would also physically chastise us — with belts, shoes, water hoses, switches, brooms, fist, feet, extension cords, and whatever else she could use to whup us. Back then, I thought that whuppings were okay. Those were the tools that she was taught, as far as raising children. It's part of the culture in the South — we didn't look at it as abuse.

I was unhappy as a child and later realized I had been dealing with depression my entire life. At the age of sixteen I smoked my first blunt (a combination of pot and cigars). That was the same age I attempted suicide. I really thought that I wanted to die.

My relationship with my father was non-existent. Maybe that's why I became so sexually active in high school. I would have sex with anyone who showed me attention. I barely graduated.

I was raped three different times, all within a two-year span. I was raped by a serial rapist when I was almost 19. This guy had been raping a lot of women in the neighborhood. After it happened, my mom told me to go to school and not tell anyone. (I finally saw a picture of that rapist in 2011, when they convicted him. He had been paroled for good behavior back in the 70s, after being imprisoned for rape and supposedly serving two life sentences.) The second time I was raped, some guys drugged me. They got scared that they had given me too much, so they left me behind the dumpster. They dumped alcohol all over me, so whoever found me would think I was drunk. The girl who found me called the police, who called the coroner. He woke me up with smelling salts. The police refused to press charges, because they said I didn't know where I had been. I couldn't remember exactly what had happened.

In my early twenties I began snorting cocaine, drinking alcohol, and had too many sexual partners to count. After a particularly abusive relationship, I decided I wanted a better life. I fled Florida while 8½ months pregnant with my third child. My two children were in the car with me. It was December 5, 2007, and I was determined to get out of that state. With only $300 dollars to my name, my choices were limited. I could go stay with a friend in Georgia or go farther and stay with a friend in Massachusetts. When I arrived in Georgia, my instincts told me to keep going. I just didn't feel far enough away. Safety was a huge factor for me, and Georgia felt too close to my abuser. I kept driving.

We made it to Virginia when I decided to stop and rest at a motel because of the weird stuff coming out the sky. That weird stuff turned out to be snow flurries. Being lifelong Floridians we had never seen snow before. My children were captivated by its beauty. Northerners may associate snow with shoveling, plowing, and delayed travel plans, but to me snow is a symbol of restoration—of a new life and a new beginning.

First Encounters With Love

"I think you're learning to mother yourself."
— Sherry

"So many of you haven't had a chance to be playful, free, secure, and full of wonder."
— Carole

Women who have experienced family violence during childhood are more susceptible to entering an abusive relationship as adults. Other family experiences can also contribute to increased susceptibility. Certainly, through our relationships with our families, we develop our sense of self and autonomy. We learn about intimacy, about whether or not the world is a safe place, and what to expect from relationships.

Children who are exposed to adverse childhood experiences are at increased risk for multiple health problems — including Intimate Partner Violence. However, this is not the whole picture. Ultimately, perpetrators of Intimate Partner Violence are responsible for the abuse they inflict, and they do not discriminate — preying both on people who had safe, nurturing childhood experiences and those who did not.

> The Adverse Childhood Experiences Study, a long-term, collaborative study between the Centers for Disease Control and Prevention and Kaiser Permanente, looks at the lifelong impact of chronic stress and trauma in childhood. The study has shown that stresses, such as witnessing or experiencing domestic abuse as a child, can lead to "a constellation of chronic conditions in adulthood." Indeed, children who witness abuse in their families are at an increased risk for abusive relationships in adulthood because they "have grown up learning that violence is normal behavior."

Tonight, the women share memories of their early childhood experiences of love and safety, or lack thereof. Donna-Marie kicks things off by reading a poem she wrote about the abuse she experienced as a child.

BLOW

Standing at the bottom
Don't even know my worth.
I'm shaking my head
Because this world doesn't even
Know what it has birthed.
I'm half out of my mind,
Trying to be one of a kind.
But instead I fall victim to
The vicious words you said.
I feel the blows with no regret
And I'm left to wonder what else will I get.

You say you love me, and then another blow
But each time you hit your face starts to glow.
Glow with the excitement of giving me pain
Glow with anticipation from making my face rain.
There you go just as you always do,
Leaving me on the floor and me watching your back as
you walk out the door.

— **Donna-Marie**

Donna-Marie's voice quavers as she reads, and there is not a peep among the women once she finishes. It is Donna-Marie herself who breaks the silence and begins to share some childhood memories.

Donna-Marie: The message in my home was, because I love you, I'm going to beat your ass. Most of the times when I got a beating it was because of something I did in school or at home. When I got a beating for doing something bad, the next day in school I'd just sit there because I was hurting so much. The day after, when I felt a little better, I'd act out again—I wouldn't listen, or I'd just get up and walk out of the classroom, or take a swing at a teacher. It didn't really matter what I did; it was just to get a reaction. I was so hurt and angry, I wanted someone else to feel my pain. It was a cry for help, but nobody heard it.

My mother would beat me because the kitchen wasn't clean enough or because I looked at her funny or because I didn't mop the floor well enough. In my house, if you didn't respond, you were being fresh. If you did respond, you were being rude or ignorant. You couldn't do anything right. The message was, "I am bigger than you. I am powerful. You are nothing."

My dad was my spoiler, but he didn't protect me. He'd protect her, his wife (my mother) above everything. If he didn't agree, he would still support her. They presented a united front—they sided together above all else.

The only person who never beat me and really talked to me was my grandmother. She was really stern, old school. She believed in church, above all. She took me on trips. In her own way, she knew the beatings were getting to me. The trips were like a reprieve. She believed in me, believed I could be better. She saw something in me. She invested in me. She was a teacher and was getting her Master's Degree at Boston College. She was the oldest woman in her class! She used to take me to the library with her when she would study. That's why I went on to become a teacher.

Selma: I'm of Hispanic descent and later realized I was very sheltered. For example, when I first went into Boston to visit a friend, I got off at the subway station with my two older children and was so petrified I ran to a cop and asked him to please help me get out of there. I was so ignorant because I really was never exposed to anything outside of my family's world. That was the reason I grabbed on to the man who turned out to be my abuser, because he opened my eyes to a larger world.

Becca: I was always expected to do well and achieve. I was once grounded for a whole summer for getting a C+ in math in high school. That was the first C I'd ever gotten. It was about living up to my family's standards and expectations and not really forming any of my own. That's bullshit. Expectations were high, but nobody ever provided guidance on how to achieve those expectations.

Growing up, I had no sense of self. I was not Becca. If I didn't get an A, the message was: "You didn't get the A, *and* you're a piece of shit." It was awful. And effective. When they told me that, I believed it. I still had a love of learning, but it wasn't about my own self-actualization. I wish it had been, because I do have that now. But I did well in school simply because there were terrific repercussions if I didn't. When I did do well, somebody would give me a dollar for my efforts. Losing was a huge thing, and winning was just expected.

I was sheltered, too. I wasn't allowed to have a black friend. When I brought a black friend home from school, she wasn't allowed into my house; she had to wait on the sidewalk. I didn't understand then, but I do now.

Donna-Marie: I had my own bond with people who became my family. That's how I began to learn what love is. I developed a lot of relationships with people at church and in school. I had a friend—Johnny. We were inseparable. We were like brother and sister. We'd get into trouble, and his mother wouldn't do anything to him. She'd yell at the school and take him home. My mother would come to the school and yell at *me*. I knew that when Johnny went home, he was safe. He knew that when I went home, I wasn't safe.

It was an "aha" moment to realize what went on in other families. I saw other families love each other and wished we had that. I was jealous, but also insecure about love—I didn't know what love meant. Love was pain for me.

Carole: In some cases, your families weren't there. It's one thing to lose that care and support, it's another when you never had it. So many of you haven't had a chance to be playful, free, secure, and full of wonder.

Olive: My grandfather was the person who really believed in me. I was everything to him. Everything. I think about him a lot. He stands out more than my own father or mother. He was just so special. Every Friday night he would take me to Mrs. Morton's restaurant, and we'd get fried chicken and corned beef. Our father wouldn't let us go anywhere, but my grandfather would take us out, and he'd let us see our friends. He was a big old bear.

I have vivid memories of the way he walked, his car, the sound of his voice. His backyard was right next to my house. I can still see the flowers in the yard and hear him talking to me from the window. I'd be outside hanging up the sheets, and he'd come out and play with me. There wasn't a day without him. He'd give me special treats. He taught me to swim. He believed in me. They all did, but he was just my rescuer, my savior. He passed away after I came to Boston. I couldn't get back to the Caribbean for the funeral.

I dreamt about him the night he died. In my dream, I was a little girl of four or five, wearing little overalls and standing outside with the clothespins. He didn't say anything, but I feel like he was with me when he died. I called my grandpa "DaDa." He took me back to a place of innocence. I really miss him. If he were still alive, I think I'd be more secure.

Becca: My family didn't care about me. It's really as simple as that. When I was 19, I had my son, and I placed him for adoption at birth with a family, in an open adoption. That was the final straw with my family. My mother had told me I should have an abortion. They completely disowned me.

After being homeless for a number of years, I remember calling my mom when I received my Section 8 housing and finally got a place, but it was my brother who came over to help me move in. He took me to the store and bought me $200 worth of groceries and helped me "furnish" the place with a few spoons and bowls. I was pregnant with my daughter at the time.

He noticed my abuser, who was also my daughter's father, in the house, and the last thing he said to me was "Get rid of him." Then he got in his car and sped away.

Selma: Sometimes I think it's not that our families don't care; it's that they don't understand.

Cecilia: I was away from my family. I had no friends. I just wanted somebody to love me. That's all I wanted.

Allison: That's what everyone wants. We just chose the wrong assholes.

Becca: It's weird for me even to see a sitcom on TV without feeling like I'm grieving, like I've missed out on something. I couldn't let myself hurt then. I was too busy surviving. But it hurts now. I want to give my family the benefit of the doubt, but at this point it is futile. If I could write to them, it would get out a lot of anger, but they wouldn't read it. I don't think my family is evil. I just think they're sick.

Carole: You cut off relationships that don't feed you.

Selma: I think you have to educate people.

Allison: My family has the same code. I don't get emotional support from my brothers and sisters. It wasn't until last year that my older sister acknowledged that she was even aware that I'd been raped twice. In fact, I'd been raped three times, but they only knew about two. The acknowledgement came too late. I needed the support *then*. But because of the family code, she couldn't acknowledge it. She said, "I always wanted to tell you that I'm proud of you."

When I left Florida, I wasn't just fleeing my abuser. I was fleeing everything.

When I was raped in high school, I was left behind a dumpster. My dad didn't speak to me for six months. He was angry with me. He felt that if I hadn't skipped school that day it wouldn't have happened.

If I had to do it over again, I'd try not to grow up so quickly, to enjoy being a child while I still was one. My mom had a 9th-grade education, my dad a 3rd-grade one. I was deputized to be the "adult" of the family. *I* was the one in charge of filling out paperwork, doing research, and answering questions. I had to forge my dad's signature on his social security checks.

I looked for compliments from men on the street, because I wasn't getting them at home. I tell my daughter every day how beautiful she is. I want her to have a partner who complements her, not one she feels has to validate her.

Becca: My family has never been there for me. And they're not there for me now. My mother missed my daughter's birthday party because she was upset with me. My mom has borderline personality disorder, so either you're all good or you're all evil. This year I was all evil. She wants me to pay emotionally, but she's also trying to make my daughter pay. I'm not letting it happen. I'm done with my mother. She was the last holdout of my whole family. I wanted to have compassion for her mental illness, because I have Post-Traumatic Stress Disorder, but I can't allow her to abuse me anymore.

Post Traumatic Stress Disorder (PTSD) is a condition of persistent mental and emotional stress occurring as a result of injury or severe psychological shock.

The National Center for PTSD lists four main symptoms of PTSD:

1. Reliving the event through nightmares, disassociation, flashbacks, and sensory triggers

2. Avoiding situations that remind you of the event

3. Negative changes in beliefs—thinking about yourself differently because of the trauma—feeling guilty, fearful, shamed; losing interest in things you once enjoyed

4. Feeling keyed up and hyper-vigilant—jittery, always alert and on the lookout for danger; difficulty concentrating or sleeping

She never was the mother that I needed or wanted. She never could be. She never did anything to protect us from the rest of the family. She was just so ill. I really want to have compassion for her, and I do in a lot of ways, but the compassion ends when the abuse starts. I learned that through the domestic violence situation. I was way too compassionate with my abuser and with a lot of men prior to that. I can't let another person abuse me that way. So my mother's on the back burner now. I'm not demonizing her, it's just that I've come to realize she's not a healthy component of the life that I want. She was the catalyst for a lot of the shit that happened to me.

Olive: Some relationships just don't happen.

Becca: It never happened. I'm grieving the loss of my mother, a mother that I never had to begin with. I can't allow her to treat my daughter the same way she treated me. And that's what she's doing, *de facto*. I cannot bear witness to that and not do anything.

Selma: You are breaking the cycle by being the mother that you are today.

Becca: Thank you. I appreciate that. My mother wasn't strong enough to break the cycle.

Sherry: What's amazing to me is that you didn't have the kind of mother you needed, yet you know how to be a great mother for Kayla. You are all changing the patterns of your families and your history.

Becca: I don't know how that happened. I don't know if it's something from the divine or what. I knew exactly what I *didn't* want to happen. I was 19 when my son was born, and I knew that I wanted him to have a better life, so I gave him up for adoption. I was in such a vulnerable position. As for Kayla, I knew she needed a mother who would be there for her, and that's what I'm giving her. I'm not like my mother. I'm doing exactly the opposite of what she did. Screw that lifestyle.

I have finally come to accept that my family has never been there for me and never will be. That's just the way it is. For the longest time I didn't accept it. I fell into a lot of traps because I so desperately wanted it to be different.

Carole: It amazes me that somehow you grew up with all of those negative influences in your life, and yet you have developed such integrity and such values. You're such a strong and amazing woman.

Becca: Thank you.

Sherry: I think you're learning to mother yourself.

Becca: I have to. Nobody else is going to do it. Actually, the people around me now are nurturing me and helping to empower me, which is nice. That feels better. But I'm taking care of myself.

Donna-Marie: We're surrounding ourselves with more positive people. I'd never been close to women before this group. It was me and the guys. We could have a brawl and then be friends. I thought women meant drama. Here, ultimately, we're each responsible for the choices we make. We have to love each other and care about each other, even if one of us makes a bad choice. I wouldn't leave any of you. That's what happened when people abused us. I won't do that.

Being with more positive people helps us be better mothers. We want to change our children's lives; we don't want them to have ours.

False First Impressions

"I was 'BooBoo the Fool.' I thought I could rescue him."
— Allison

There is something intoxicating about the early days of a relationship. It's fabulous to love someone and to feel loved in return. In that heightened emotional state, it is natural to want the euphoria to continue and easy to overlook or make excuses for behavior that suggests that all may not be right in paradise. It helps to know the warning signs.

According to Lundy Bancroft in *Why Does He Do That?*, you know you are in an abusive relationship when:

- Your partner is disrespectful toward you.

- Your partner speaks disrespectfully of his former partners, blaming them for all of the problems.

- Your partner is controlling and possessive.

- Your partner does favors for you that you don't want or makes you uncomfortable with shows of generosity.

- Your partner pressures you for sex, is forceful or scary regarding sex.

- Your partner gets too serious about the relationship too fast.

- Your partner abuses drugs or alcohol.

- Your partner blames you for the abusive behavior, saying you provoked it, or brought it on yourself.

- Your partner believes that men should be in control and powerful and that women should be passive and submissive.

- Your partner is intimidating when angry.

- Your partner appears to be attracted to vulnerability.

- Your partner is self-centered.

- Your partner treats you differently when around other people.

- Your partner isolates you from friends and family.

The discussion topic for this evening is the early days of the relationship and the women's initial impressions of the person who turned out to be their abuser. It is a somber subject, but the discussion begins with some good news from Selma, who is checking in by phone. Her news comes out in one big rush. "Big news," she says. "I just started my new job. I'm the office manager for a property management team. The owner is a multi-millionaire. I'm doing accounts payable. The pay and benefits are great. I will have so much more financial stability. I won't have to be all over the place anymore. I started work yesterday. I have to wear heels everyday! The rest of you guys, hang in there. It will get better."

There is much cheering and clapping around the table. The group is so proud of Selma's accomplishment and so happy for this new beginning in her life. The women take a collective moment to bask in Selma's good news before turning their attention to the topic at hand.

Each abusive situation is unique in its own way, but as the women brainstorm a list of the first impressions they had of their abusers, they realize there are many common themes. There is much emphatic nodding around the table as the women shout out phrases to complete the sentence Carole has written on the whiteboard: "I thought he was. . ."

- So beautiful. So amazing. So handsome, charming, charismatic, and respectful.

- My soul mate, my protector.

- He promised me the world when I had nothing.

- He promised me we would have a beautiful family.

- He said he loved me.

But then . . .

- He poked a hole in the condom.

- He isolated me, humiliated me, robbed and beat me, and took control over my whole world.

- He made sure the only person I had in my life was him.

> In *The Batterer as Parent*, Lundy Bancroft lists these common characteristics of an abuser:
>
> - Controlling
> - Entitled
> - Selfish / self-centered
> - Feels superior
> - Possessive
> - Confuses love and abuse
> - Manipulative
> - Demonstrates contradictory statements and behaviors
> - Externalizes responsibility
> - Denies, minimizes, and blames victim
> - Engages in serial battering

Cecilia: I met my abuser on the Boston T (subway), which I had to take every day. He worked for the MBTA as a police officer. He used to come up to me and talk to me, and I was so shy I would keep backing up and backing up until I was pressed up against the side of the subway car.

Shortly after I met him, the family I was living with went home to Mexico. They would not take me home with them. I was on my own. I was barely making it. I was barely making money. I only spoke broken English, and I was living with people who were stealing from me. They stole everything. There was no privacy in the house. I was waking up with nightmares. Where was I going to go? Every night I was very scared. When I would see the sun, I would know I'd made it through one more day. I'd think: "I'm OK."

I wanted to feel loved. I didn't like the idea of being alone and scared. I didn't feel safe. As a girl, you dream about the prince who will come and love you, this perfect man who loves you just the way you are. I thought that I had found him.

I'd never had a boyfriend before. I was so young, and he was twelve years older. I really felt that I was lucky. He was tall, strong, and an American. He wore nice uniforms and had a very important job. I felt intelligent because he was a native English speaker. I thought he was smart, and it made me feel smart and important to be with him.

He always took me places where nobody else was around. On our first date, he took me fishing. I felt beautiful, but scared. I wanted to be a grown up, but I was young—still too young to go drinking in the bars.

He forced me to have sex. I didn't want to, but I knew that by agreeing to go to his home, I was asking for it.

> In her book, *Invisible Chains: Overcoming Coercive Control in Your Intimate Relationships*, Lisa Aronson Fontes, Ph.D., states: Coerced sex is humiliating and extremely common in abusive relationships. Further, abusers often feel stronger when making their partners feel powerless and ashamed.

I tied my sweatpants as tight as I could so he couldn't get them off, but he tore them off. Afterward, he laughed and said: "I can't believe you let me."

At this point, the group collectively interjects, everyone doing her best to inform Cecilia that what had happened was, in fact, rape.

Then I got pregnant and he told me to move in with him. I felt I had to. Once there, I felt like I went to hell. I told my mom I wanted to come home to Mexico, but she wouldn't let me. She said my father would be upset because I had a child. If I went home, she said I'd have to leave my daughter behind. I couldn't leave my child. I would rather live and suffer with him than leave my child. As hard as it was, I had to stay to be with my daughter.

> Escalation of violence during pregnancy is common. Abusers often resent that a child is coming into the picture and will draw attention away from them and their needs. In fact, The University of California San Francisco Medical Center cites domestic violence as the most common health problem among women during pregnancy.

At home, I became only a little bit more than a slave.

When my daughter was older, he told her that I was an airhead and that the only reason he wanted to have a child with me was because I was so pure. He used me to have a child. I thought he was honest like I was.

Allison: I was set up with this guy. Even before we met, we spent hours on the phone talking about the Bible. He used that as a tool to capture me. He told me a bit about his criminal record, but he didn't go into detail. He didn't reveal that he was investigated for attempted murder in Miami and for arson.

He *did* tell me he was investigated for a murder in Orlando—he turned to me and said, "I don't mind killin' a bitch." I was "Boo Boo the Fool." I thought I could rescue him.

The first two weeks with him were great. But on the third day of knowing him, he had the gall to ask me what day I received my paycheck. That should have told me everything I needed to know. He would follow me to the bank and ask me for money. I should have run!

Olive: I was a happy, self-sufficient girl who had my life planned. I was on my way to doing what I wanted: pursuing my degree in biology and planning to go to medical school. I was parenting my daughter as a single mother, holding down a job and taking care of us financially.

When I first met him everything was completely normal. We became friends and began dating. We did all the things that couples do. We went out for dinner, to the movies, and took weekend trips together. Our relationship flourished. I was so in love with him and was certain that he was the right guy for me. When we had mild disagreements, I conceded. It was in my nature to avoid conflict.

Selma: My guy was so foreign from anyone I had ever known. He was incredibly charismatic, with this real ability to communicate and pull people toward him. I met him through a friend. He was from the south, the youngest of his large family, and had lived overseas for a bit. He had the nice car and the fancy clothes. He was very handsome: 6' 2", athletic, broad-shouldered, trim, a great dresser.

He taught me to embrace my heritage. He embraced my world of the arts and showed me museums and passion and rose petals. He really showed me the world. We could go anywhere together and fit right in—from a scummy, hole-in-the-wall bar to a black-tie gala. The more I became engrossed in his world, the more my world fell away. I thought it was loving and embracing. It wasn't until later that I realized it was isolating.

The relationship was beautiful for years, but everything changed once our son was born. Now I call that man "Rodent."

Becca: When I first met him I was homeless, living in a transitional living shelter for homeless youth and working full time. As a requirement of living in the house, I had to attend Alcoholics Anonymous (AA) meetings. What I really needed was a co-dependency program. I met him at one of those AA meetings. He was 20; I was 21. He was Native American, and he came across as a really nice person. Pretty quickly he started showing up at my work, and I'd hand over everything I had made in tips—usually about $35/day.

Allison: I don't think it's coincidence that he learned about your job and your income that first time you met him.

Becca: He eventually found out about my savings, too. He started brainwashing me about the transitional living program and tried to turn me against it. When I had $2,000 saved, he asked me to leave the program to be with him, even though he, too, was homeless.

I got pregnant with Kayla that winter. I went back and forth to different shelters. I had a locker in one place and would shower at another. On cold nights, we would sleep in the storeroom where I worked, on an icy concrete floor, without anyone knowing.

I lost my job in May because my pregnancy made it unsafe for me to lift the heavy milk crates anymore. It was brutal.

Selma: Did you ever love him?

Becca: I didn't know what love was. I equated it with affection. And he was attentive. So I guess for some part of me, yes, I thought that was love.

Donna-Marie: My false first impression was that the woman who turned out to be my abuser was the same person I had known as a child. I didn't realize how much she had changed from the person I had known long ago. I ran into her at Stop & Shop (a grocery store), after being out of touch with her for years. We reminisced about the past and talked about relationships. We had been inseparable as kids. Our friendship was based around church. In some ways we had totally different backgrounds. She had all sisters, I had all brothers, but both of our mothers were mean and aggressive. We both experienced lots of verbal and physical abuse.

> According to the World Health Organization, domestic violence is learned behavior; it is learned through multiple sources, including observation, personal experience, culture, family of origin, communities, school, and friends.

She was violent, but not towards me, not at the beginning. I didn't care. I felt that she had had a harder life than I did. I felt more compassion for her than I did for myself. I remember thinking I could love her through her hurt and pain.

It's Complicated

"I gave him a life vest without putting mine on first. I couldn't conceptualize how far he would go and how isolating it would be. The excuses. The shame. The embarrassment. It doesn't go away."

— Becca

"It was all so complicated, so overwhelming, and I was too scared to tell."

— Olive

In the course of informal conversations outside of the circle, the women realized that they'd each made excuses for their abusers and had made similar attempts to try to salvage their relationships. As the women give voice to their feelings, Carole once again tacks paper to the walls of the conference room and writes frantically, trying to keep up with the outpouring of words.

I felt . . .

- So alone. How could I make it without him?
- I had to keep my family together, my career on track.
- I couldn't let my secret out.
- I thought I was the only one.
- I felt numb.
- I felt like I couldn't tell anybody.
- Someone else was living my life for me.
- I lost myself.
- I felt hopeless.
- I existed for him.
- I felt like all the problems were my fault.
- I felt trapped with no way out.

- If I tried harder, things would get better.
- If I tried harder, I would be good enough for him.
- I told secrets and lies to cover up what I was doing, as much as what he was doing.
- I lied to myself that I could fix her.
- I made her feel up while I felt down.
- I kept secrets from him, hiding everything — money, credit cards, phone.
- I couldn't say who I had been with or talking to.

Page after page gets filled, and there seems to be catharsis in the process. Carole's arm gives out before the words do, but there's no need to continue. The point has been made.

Allison: I felt embarrassed. That's why I wouldn't say anything to anyone. Even if my parents had been alive, I know I would not have told them. They would have told me that I should have known better.

> In *50 Obstacles to Leaving*, Sarah Buel states: Survivors stay in relationships for many reasons, including fear for their safety, shame, financial dependency, fear of losing child custody, and economic reality. There may also be family and cultural pressure to stay and guilt that it is because of their incompetent and faulty behavior that they are being abused.

I tried to get him out of my life, but I also tried to hide the relationship from my family. I excluded everyone. No one, not my friends nor my siblings, knew I was in an abusive relationship. Anthony would use slaps to control me, and at one point my sister voiced her opinion that this man was not the person she thought he was. Rather than confessing the truth, I got defensive. "Everyone has faults," I said to her. "Who are you to judge?"

Becca: I lied to everybody about him. He lived in my apartment with me and didn't work. He had no income and drank everyday. He went to the midwife appointments with me, but he didn't want the midwife to know he was the father. He put on this flamboyant act and told everyone he was my gay friend. And he played the part to the hilt. He was so afraid of having to pay child support, I had to deny to everyone that he was the father. I went to church and lied to everyone right there in church. "No, he's not the father," was my standard response when people asked, even though she looked just like him.

Looking back at that time, I realize that I gave him a life vest without putting mine on first. I couldn't conceptualize how far he would go and how isolating it would be. The excuses. The shame. The embarrassment. It doesn't go away. It's like that game, Jenga. Each piece comes out one by one, and the structure gets more and more hollow, until the whole thing collapses.

Cecilia: There were days he was nice. When his family was there he would kiss and hug me. But it wasn't true. I heard him say to his brother: "I have to train her." His brother responded: "She doesn't seem like a bad girl. You shouldn't touch her." To which he replied: "I have to. I'm a man."

In my heart, I just wanted him to love me, so I stayed with him for many years. Now I don't care about him at all. I think you have to forgive the people who hurt you most. I'm fine now.

Olive: I had to cover up a lot and lie when I went into court. I had to make him feel good—I wanted him to feel happy, even though it made me look like a lunatic. But I had to do it—if I didn't, I wouldn't get any peace.

I couldn't tell anyone. I had to keep my family together. It was all so complicated, so overwhelming, and I was too scared to tell. Eventually I came to the realization that this was not normal. I was a victim of domestic violence. How did this happen? I had fallen a victim to shame also.

There are many reasons why a woman may not recognize for years that she is a victim of abuse. We credit Anisha Durve, author of *The Power to Break Free*, for this list of reasons women may remain unaware:

- Insidiousness—the nature of the abuse is subtle

- Secrecy—abuser conceals motivations and disguises behavior

- Blame—tactical manipulation of blaming victim for triggering behavior

- Denial—abuser's denial of abuse, and victim's self-doubt stemming from abuser's denial

- Conditioning—adapts to abuse, which includes minimizing and/or denial

- History—may not be able to identify behavior because of lack of knowledge and/or experience with abuse

- Media—victim may not relate to extreme images and stories found online

- Hope—eternal, undying hope that things will change

- Culture—cultural norms may perpetuate the abusive dynamic

Becca: The day I went to court, I couldn't get my bra on. I was in so much pain because of his beating. So I went to court without my bra.

Donna: How could this be me? How did I get here? I just couldn't understand how I got here.

Carole: You did what you had to do to piss them off as little as possible. It's like you're managing a monster.

Selma: I protected my husband many times. When I did reach out for help, I was often belittled or simply wasn't believed. I could have had him locked up many times. I should have yelled from a mountaintop and kept yelling.

If I could go back, I would pay more attention to the alienation process — the emails that were blocked, the letters that were intercepted, the phone numbers that were changed. It was so subtle; it happened so gradually. If I had something important to do, my abuser would suddenly have something *more* important to do. It got to the point where I hardly had any communication with my family. I have a degree in psychology. I was in the field. I knew what to do. Why didn't I do it?

Cecilia: Why didn't you, if you knew so much? You had the education, why wouldn't you leave? I always thought that if I had been educated, I would never have been in this mess. But you did have the education.

Selma: Why would you ask me "Why?" How can you ask me that? If there's anything we should all understand around this table it's that it's complicated, and leaving is not easy.

> **Leaving is dangerous.** In *Why Does He Do That?*, Lundy Bancroft writes that it is not uncommon for abusers to respond to their partner leaving by:
>
> - Threatening to harm or kill you
> - Threatening to kidnap or take custody of the children
> - Threatening to cut off all financial resources, causing homelessness
> - Physically or sexually assaulting you
> - Stalking you

Carole: It's because it's not about you. It's about the abuser. It's one thing to learn it. It's another to apply it to your own life.

Allison: A college degree does not stop you from becoming a victim. Not when you're in love.

Cecilia: I thought domestic violence was only in my culture. Never in a million years did I think it could happen here.

According to the World Health Organization, "about 1 in 3 women worldwide have experienced either physical and/or sexual intimate partner violence or non-partner sexual violence in their lifetime." This varies by country and culture; for example, 15% of women in Japan and 71% of women in Ethiopia reported physical and/or sexual violence by an intimate partner in their lifetime. According to the National Network to End Domestic Violence, domestic violence affects millions of individuals throughout the country, regardless of "age, economic status, race, religion, or education," citing that 1 in 3 women in the U.S. have experienced rape, physical violence, or stalking by an intimate partner in her lifetime.

It is getting late, and at 9:00 everyone agrees that it's time to stop for the evening. But the women are nowhere near finished with this topic and promise to continue the conversation the following week.

Carole and Sherry have come up with a light-hearted activity to close out the evening. The women parade around the room balancing peacock feathers on their fingers, hug each other goodbye, and walk out the door laughing.

It's Still Complicated

*"For the longest time I only looked at him from the waist down.
All I ever saw were pants and shoes."*

— Cecilia

Last week's discussion was too big to fit into one session, so tonight the women continue to talk about the truth of their relationships and the moment when they acknowledged the abuse and their pain.

The group checks in . . .

Donna-Marie had been the keynote speaker at recent Second Step fundraising event, "Celebrating Success." She brought a crowd of more than 400 people to complete silence as she recounted the story of the abuse she endured first as a child and then as an adult. The crowd listened, rapt, as she told of the people who had helped her survive, the teachers and friends who saw something in her and looked beyond her behavior and reached out to help. She called each of them a "peg" in her journey up and away from abuse. When she concluded her speech, the crowd rose as one to applaud.

It doesn't seem like the same woman sitting here at the table today. She keeps her head down and from time to time tears slip from her eyes. The strong, vibrant woman who had stood on a podium just one week earlier has been replaced by someone vulnerable and raw.

Donna-Marie: The first time I acknowledged what was going on was when I wrote my speech for "Celebrating Success." I didn't think that I was weak. I didn't think I was vulnerable.

I didn't think I was powerless. Through writing my speech, I realized how much of a victim I was—to physical abuse, emotional abuse, psychological abuse, sexual abuse, and verbal abuse. I realized the enormity of everything I had gone through.

In my last abusive relationship, I knew I had to leave, but I didn't know why. I was getting weaker. There was the weight of the rock on top of me. I had become accustomed to the verbal putdowns, not feeling confident, second-guessing my decisions. Somehow, I knew, for me, I had to face my past.

Cecilia: After my boyfriend and I moved in together, he became a different person. The first day after I moved in with him, he sat me down to tell me what he expected from me. I thought he was joking! I didn't think it was real. But he was serious! He told me what I could wear, where I could go.

He told me I never cleaned the house right. I never did anything right. In his eyes, I was not good enough. He controlled everything: what I ate, what I wore, whether or not I could open a window. When I was allowed to leave the house, I would go for walks in the cemetery with my daughter. Before he'd let me leave the house to go to church, he would force me to change, saying my neckline was too low. When I wore make up, he would smudge my face and make me wash it off. If I tried to go for a walk, he thought I was seeing another man. He was so jealous. He told me if I ever saw somebody else, he would cut me and destroy my face.

> The dynamic Cecelia is describing is referred to as *Intimate Terrorism*. In their book, *Listening to Battered Women: A Survivor-Centered Approach to Advocacy, Mental Health, and Justice*, Lisa Goodman, Ph.D. and Deborah Epstein, JD, state that Intimate Terrorism refers to an insidious and overarching pattern of coercion and control that a perpetrator uses with his partner—control over the finances, the social contacts, parenting, employment, clothing, etc., to the point where even non-violent control tactics instill fear of potential physical harm. These power and control techniques are similar to those applied to prisoners of war in 1973, as defined by the Amnesty International Report on Torture.

He trained me to obey, not to talk back, not to look at him if he was yelling. He was an animal when he was mad! For the longest time I only looked at him from the waist down. All I ever saw were pants and shoes. If his shoes were too close to me, I would think about where I could run. It was not safe. It's how I lived.

He used to tell me: "A bag of crack cocaine to kill you." That's all it would take—the promise of a $10 bag of cocaine to get somebody to kill me.

Once he hit me so badly my nose was dripping blood, and he had the nerve to yell at me for making a mess. "You made me do this to you," he screamed. Another time he threw me down the stairs. I thought I'd die that day. He would kick me and spit in my face and choke me with my own hair.

Carole: Strangulation is the most intimate form of violence. It is a high indicator of lethality. You were in such danger. It's amazing you survived.

Cecilia: I just tried to please him and make him happy. I thought if I did what he wanted everything would be all right. But he asked me for more and more. After I had our baby, I felt fat and ugly. He gave me hateful looks. I didn't know how to please him. He started calling me names and making fun of me. I was a failure. I didn't make him happy. He would go out to drink because he said that I drove him crazy. That's what he told me; that's what I believed.

Donna-Marie: With my abuser, the violence started because she would get drunk. She would transform, become a whole different person. She would call out my name—"bitch"—and I would stay silent because I didn't want to hurt her, and I didn't like confrontation, especially arguments. She would put her finger in my face and shush me, as if to say I wasn't worth shit. She was constantly putting me down, trying to make me feel less than her. "No one will love you like me," she often said. "No one is going to put up with your bullshit." And she would constantly put down my daughter, telling me how spoiled she was. "You need to put your foot in her ass," she'd say, and then follow that with, "Why don't you beat her? She is so disrespectful." I knew I wasn't going to do that. I already knew, deep down, that she was jealous.

> According to The Minnesota Advocates for Human Rights Study, while perpetrators often blame their abusive behavior on drugs and alcohol, this is, in fact, a myth. While drugs and alcohol may lessen inhibitions, it is simply an excuse for their abusive acts.

One evening, she was so drunk she called me for a ride home but at the same time told me I wasn't worth shit and threatened to punch me in my face. I picked her up, and her sister joined us. She was trying to fight me from the back seat while her sister tried to hold her back because I was driving. When we got home, she told me to get away from her; that she didn't need my help. She was still trying to fight me, but she was sick from alcohol and couldn't hold it in.

Becca: I was living with my abuser under a bridge. Even though I was homeless, I didn't have drug or alcohol issues. It was the abuse that kept me outside. My abuser did have alcohol issues, and he relied on me to supply him with alcohol. If he didn't have it, he would get the shakes, and the abuse would be even worse.

After I found out I was pregnant, I had to keep myself safer, because I had two lives to worry about. So here I was, pregnant. I had lost my job as a supervisor at Starbucks. When money was low, he would make me go out and ask for money. I had a sign that said "homeless, pregnant, and in dire need." I would sit there for hours, and the lovely people of Boston would offer food and money, some of which I put away in a secret bank account.

I didn't have a family to turn to. I was at his mercy. I had to do what he wanted me to do, or he would have gotten violent. The sure way I could quell his violence was to make sure he had access to alcohol. I would go into a shelter on cold nights, but they weren't particularly helpful. They didn't screen for domestic violence. Even if they had, I don't know if I would have told them. I was afraid of losing my unborn baby. I had already given up a son; I didn't want to give up this second child.

He protected me on the streets, so I knew I had some degree of safety with him around. Protecting myself from people on the street was job number one, and protecting myself from him was job number two. I was twenty-two-years-old. How much more vulnerable can you be — a twenty-two-year-old pregnant woman without a home, without a family, without friends. He was all I had! I had graduated 11th in my class in high school, gone to college, and was now trying to uphold and maintain my personal dignity doing everything I could to stay alive. I lived this way for a very long time.

Allison: I remember one day in particular. I was at his mom's house sitting with him in the front yard. He had this strange grin on his face, and he kept flexing his muscles and pretending to punch me. "You know, I could take you out with one punch," he said. Another time, he had a gun, and he kept hitting my knee with it. I told him to stop before it went off. He said, "Yeah, if it goes off, I'm going to make sure it's pointing the right way." We just looked at each other — I knew what he meant.

> According to groundbreaking work by Jacqueline Campbell, an abuser's access to weapons is one predictor of a higher risk, potentially deadly situation. Other predictors of increased lethality are:
>
> - If you are planning to leave or have recently left your abuser after living with him for the past year
> - If the violence has increased in severity and/or frequency over the last year
> - If the abuser has ever attempted to strangle you
> - If the abuser has ever used a weapon against you, or threatened you with a weapon
> - If the abuser stalks you
>
> A list of resources for predicting risk can be found in the Appendix at the back of this book.

I was with him three-and-a-half months. It went downhill within the first two weeks. He had me convinced that the world was against him.

In hindsight, I was in complete denial. His ex-wife's cousin called me and played a recording of him saying he didn't love me and that he was using me for my money. I refused to acknowledge that it was his voice on the tape recorder.

Then I found out that his "ex" was still his wife. She stuck a gun in my face and said she'd blow my fucking face off. He got her strung out on dope, and he used me for money. My little one was in the car at the time.

Even so, we went to church every Sunday and to Bible study on Tuesdays.

He asked to borrow my car and promptly tried to use it to run over his wife. She lost her kids to Social Services because of him.

Olive: We planned to have a child together, and everything took a turn once I became pregnant. His fury unleashed on me. There are so many violent examples that I have in my mind. Too many to mention: a bruised body and a bruised mind; shredded passports. I was broken into many different pieces. I can remember riding in police cars to the hospital with my legs bruised and my face slashed. I remember his boots bruising my sides when he pushed me into a closet. There was no place I could go to get away.

> **Once again, Olive's experience is reflective of how violence can escalate during pregnancy.**

If I hadn't been careful I would have had six children by him by now. It was relentless. I was his possession. It was my job to have the kids, but I couldn't sit and have dinner with them. He wouldn't let me join them at the table. I was like an outcast.

When my oldest son was born, I broke my pelvic bone. For a long time, I couldn't get out of bed. He knocked me off of my crutches after weeks of physical therapy, and I got reinjured. I had to go the hospital, but I denied that he had hurt me. I had to be back in bed. I was dependent on him. I couldn't move myself.

He would leave me alone with my baby all day. He would pick me up and put me down on the toilet so hard that I'd scream. He'd leave my milk, food, diapers, and wipes by the bed so I could manage during the day. I would call him at work to help me, and he would tell me to manage.

There were times he called the police saying I stole his car. In truth, he was the one who stole the car, multiple times. But it was his name on the title, not mine. The police would pull me over, and I could tell they felt so bad because I had two little boys in the car.

After my daughter (my third child) was born, it occurred to me that I was simply a vehicle for his children. Anytime I bought something for myself, he'd say, "I hope you spent as much on the kids. They have to have as much or better than you."

PART II

GET HELP:
Finding The Strength
To Reach Out

Whispers From A Sister

Your silence is not suiting you.   **Shelter is an option.**

Note the glimmers of grace on even the worst days.

Sometimes it gets worse before it gets better.

IT'S NOT EASY.

Stop caring for people who judge you. Don't let them pull you down.

Create a cover for yourself, a way to feel protected.

Not everyone who tries to help you navigate the system will be on the up and up. Find the right people to help you.

Stay focused on what's best for you and your family.

A plan is always good.   BE CAREFUL WHO YOU TRUST.

Pick and choose your battles. Know what you're willing to fight for and what you're willing to give up.

Visualize the light at the end of the tunnel. Even if you can't see it, believe that it's there.

Stay positive. Keep fighting.   Watch your back.

A shelter is not a resort, it's a last resort.

Plan for your safety. Set achievable, small, realistic goals.

Don't let the shelter become your life. Create a network both inside and outside the shelter.

It's complicated.   Heroes come in all sizes, shapes, and colors.

Thinking About Leaving

"A good friend told me, 'When you've had enough, you'll know.'"
— Selma

"The first time I called the hotline, I was so scared that I hung up."
— Cecilia

There is a new face in the group tonight. Amber had been active in the Narrative Healing Group a few years earlier, but was sidelined due to illness. She is back, and there is a decidedly uncertain mood in the room. Will she fit in? How can the women open up to her when she hasn't been there for the last 18 months to hear their stories, to bear witness to their tears?

But the women want to be welcoming. They, who are all about community and acceptance, are determined to rise to this challenge. Even so, there is a definite undercurrent of tension and it lasts the duration of the session.

The group checks in . . .

The question for the group today is, "How did you decide to leave?" It is immediately met with resistance. "Not everyone is able to leave," a few of the women are quick to say. Others express that it was not one "ah ha" moment that propelled them out the door. It turns out that leaving — or choosing to stay — is nuanced.

In fact, leaving is the most dangerous time. Because the dynamic of these relationships is about power and control, when a survivor makes the decision to leave and begins to take back her power, the abuser often becomes more violent, escalating his attempts to control her. The statistics bear repeating: In the course of a lifetime, one in three women will experience abuse. This abuse is an equal-opportunity epidemic affecting people across communities and nationalities; it transcends religion, race, gender presentation, age, and financial status. In addition to the obvious trauma from abuse, the Center for Disease Control (CDC) tells us that domestic violence survivors are far more likely to experience long-term, recurring health issues such as heart disease, asthma, sexual promiscuity, and substance abuse.

Abuse is not just about physical contact. More broadly, it is about manipulation, where one person uses coercion to gain control over another. If you even think you *might* be experiencing abuse, then likely you are.

As the women start to riff on the challenges of leaving an abusive relationship, their words tumble out in rapid-fire succession:

- You have to build the courage to tell someone.

- Find someone to feel safe with, that you can trust to tell.

- I shared my story with a therapist, and she said I must have done something to cause his behavior.

- It wasn't until someone noticed and said something to me that I eventually came to the realization that there was something terribly wrong, that I was being abused.

- I didn't accept help, because I thought I could fix him myself. Until he almost killed me.

- I was in situations where I thought I would live or die, and then I would run. But I didn't get the right help. Eventually I had to keep going back to him.

- When I reached out for help, I felt so judged. I needed somewhere to go, somewhere safe, where I wasn't blamed or judged.

- Reaching out for help was humiliating. I needed to find a place that wasn't abusive.

- I needed to find a place that could give me the right support.

- Many well-meaning people don't understand abuse; they make less of the situation, while other people just don't care.

- It's really hard to just walk away.

- You have to deal with lots of bureaucracy, and you become a number and begin to be treated like a number.

- You finally agree to accept help and then learn that you don't qualify for it.

- You don't really believe you can survive on your own.

- You have lost a close connection to your family, to your place in society.

- You have tremendous guilt over what is best for your children and guilt over taking them away from their other parent.

- Sometimes your abuser winds up being your only support. Your abuser becomes your rescuer. We come to believe we need to be rescued, that we need someone to take care of us.

Amber: I tried *not* to leave. I was someone who worked in this field as a social worker and daycare provider. Frankly, I was embarrassed. Who could I tell? Who would believe me? I was such a big mouth; *no way* was I a candidate for domestic violence. But he caught me at a vulnerable moment in my life, and I stayed with him out of embarrassment. I knew the Power and Control Wheel. I worked in the community. I lived a double life for years, speaking out about domestic violence and even helping two of my daycare moms break free.

I became an expert on makeup, and hid every bit of the abuse until finally I'd had enough. I called the police and had him arrested. I worked closely with the district attorney. I was told he would get three years of jail time. I remember going to court, so excited that I was going to be rid of this man. But as it turned out, he only got a $1,000 fine and mandatory anger management classes. I had to drive back home in the car with him! It was then that I realized no one was going to help me. I had policemen in my family, for heaven's sake, but I knew I was going to have to help myself.

Finally, I told my friends what had been happening, and they helped me put together my escape plan. I slowly started pulling things together. I collected the kids' school and medical records and hid them in the paperwork I kept for my daycare business. Friends collected empty moving boxes for me. I kept working and saved every penny I could and converted the money into travelers' checks. When I got to $15,000, I knew the day to leave had arrived.

Amber is describing making a safety plan in preparation to leave. Because leaving is the most dangerous time, and violence often escalates, making a safety plan prior to leaving can be a very important component of staying safe. Crisis center advocates can work with survivors to make a safety plan, creating a strategy that helps a survivor to reduce harm while in the relationship, while in the process of leaving the relationship, and after having left. A safety plan is specific to each unique situation. See Appendix for an in-depth safety check list and planning guide.

I waited for him to head off to work, and then I called my friends. They all came over with the boxes they'd saved for me, and in three hours flat we packed up that house. I left him his beloved Tupperware. I picked up my kids from the Boys & Girls Club, and we started our drive to Florida.

Somehow I knew I had to go far away. I think that's the key to escaping—going far enough away that you can't go back when things get tough, when you get lonely, when money gets tight.

Cecilia: It took me forever to get out of my first abusive relationship. I don't know how I did. He kicked me out because I didn't have the rent money. He had been out drinking, and at three o'clock in the morning he smashed the door open and yelled, "Where's the rent money? If you don't have it, you have to get out." He pushed me out. I grabbed my daughter, but he said, "No, she stays." So I went to my car. I'll never forget the sight of my daughter standing at the window, looking down at me hiding in the car and crying.

> In Cecilia's case, the abuser is responding by taking her daughter and cutting off all financial resources, thus creating homelessness.

The only way I could be safe and still be close to my daughter was to sleep outside in my car. It was the middle of winter in Boston and so cold I thought I'd freeze in place. I'd get up many times during the night to turn the car on for a bit of warmth. I'd get so cold my knees would ache and the clothes I had to wear to work the next day would freeze. In the morning, I'd go to the YMCA to get dressed, put on frozen clothes, go into work, and smile.

I used to look up at the stars through the car's rear window and pretend I was sleeping in a greenhouse. In fact, that's what my daughter and I called it. We'd talk about "the greenhouse" like we were talking about the YMCA, so nobody would know our secret.

I would sneak back into the house at night to use the bathroom, and my daughter would say: "Mommy, be quiet. If he hears you, he'll kill you." Once I had to hide under the bed when I heard him in the hall. I couldn't move a muscle. I was so scared I would sneeze or make a noise. As terrible as it was, I felt I had no choice. I couldn't take living with him anymore, and I couldn't just up and leave my daughter.

This is an example of parentification, broadly defined as any time a child takes on the responsibility of caring for the parent and the parent depends on the child for support. Parentification commonly surfaces in domestic violence situations. In Cecelia's case, her child feels responsible for her mom's safety. In general, parentification is a kind of role reversal that makes the child feel obliged to meet a parent's emotional and physical needs, and may include an expectation that the child take responsibility for the needs of younger siblings and tasks such as cooking, and cleaning.

Allison: I knew from the very beginning of the relationship that I was going to leave. After the first two weeks of courting, I realized that this man was a big-ass liar! He began to control me, to manipulate me, and then to threaten bodily harm.

One day he disappeared with my car, saying he was going to the grocery store. After three hours, I realized he hadn't gone to the grocery store. A friend suggested I check my bank account. I saw that money had been taken out. He'd gotten my pin number from watching behind my back when I withdrew money.

My friend drove me to his sister's neighborhood to look for my car. Sure enough, I found my car. There happened to be police officers nearby, and I asked them for help. Together, we went to Anthony's wife's house so I could get the car keys.

We weren't in that house for more than a minute when the police officers, who knew just what this place was, looked at my arms to check that they were clean. "You really don't know what's going on here, do you?" they asked me. Then the police officer made the others in the house show me their arms. I almost threw up. I had no idea that the house was actually a drug den.

He saw that my car was new and learned that I had a good job. He told me, "You seem to have a good head on your shoulders. You need to get rid of this deadweight." The officer asked why I was with Anthony, and I couldn't answer. I guess I kept trying to save him.

Donna-Marie: That cape keeps getting bigger and bigger.

Carole: He must have known that about you.

Allison: I tried to end the relationship in a public place. We got into a terrible fight at a restaurant, and he took my car keys from me. I told the waitress to call 9-1-1, and, when she didn't, I tried slipping her a note. But she was clueless. Thankfully, the cook saw what was going on. He came out and had the waitress walk me to the bathroom and lock me inside to keep me safe. The waitress made the call and then brought me the phone in the bathroom so the police could talk to me. The police came, and, while they couldn't hold him on any charges, they said they could at least give me a running head start. He then threatened me, and they charged him on verbal assault. So he did end up going to jail. This all happened 50 feet away from my job. I didn't go back to work that day.

That time, I ended up bailing him out because he apologized and said it wouldn't happen again. He said God had sent me to him, and he was going to make it right. But the violence didn't stop after he got out of jail. I stayed with him for another month-and-a-half, and then I moved to several different apartments to get away from him. But he always found me. Later, even when he was in jail and I was supposedly safe, his family would come and slash my tires.

The Orlando prosecutor had been pushing me to press charges for all the violence and abuse. I didn't want to press charges at first, because I just wanted the whole thing to go away. She told me the only way to make it go away would be to follow through with the charges. She told me the reason she was pushing so hard was because they needed to get him off the streets; that he had a really bad criminal record. I finally went to court, pregnant, and Anthony tried to intimidate me. We had to get three appointed guardians to sit between me and him so he couldn't talk to me.

Carole: Being in court is like being in the lion's den. There's a lot of judgment. It is not a safe place.

Allison: I went to court six times with this idiot. The first time he was charged with beating up his wife. He claimed he hadn't done it even though she had a broken nose and two black eyes — and he used my car to do it! The second time he was charged with assaulting me. The third time he convinced me to drop the charges. The fourth time he was charged with violating the "no contact" order. The fifth time he was charged with violating the emergency restraining order. The sixth, and final, time we went to court, I testified against him. He was convicted of domestic assault and sentenced to 60 days in jail. They added his drug charges to the sentence and he wound up with one year in jail.

After all that, I was done with the drama. I was tired. I was embarrassed and didn't want to be the topic of conversation at my job.

I had been telling the kids that we'd be leaving soon. My daughter was ten and my son just a toddler at the time. I started giving away my clothes to the women's shelter in Orlando and putting some of my things in storage. One day, I just woke up and was ready to leave. I handed my roommate $400 to cover the month's rent and took off. I didn't have anything but a sundress and socks and flip flops. I don't know what it was about that particular day, but I was done. I just woke up and said, "I'm out."

I left all the drama behind as I packed up my kids and my apartment and drove north on I-95. When I crossed the Florida state line, I knew I was free from him, finally. I was leaving it all behind. Not just the domestic violence, but my childhood, all of it. I couldn't heal in Florida. I had to leave the state in order to heal.

Selma: I didn't know I would leave. I was with the man more than ten years. When you have a family and a child with someone, they're supposed to protect you. A sense of survival kicks in. I was numb. You get detached. My soul had a heavy burden as I went through the motions so I could remain alive. You don't necessarily know you're going to leave in advance.

In my case, I left the day I came home from a birthday party to find our pet kitten decapitated and my son crying out, "Daddy, Daddy." It is very hard to see your child crying out. He was trembling, almost as if he craved for his dad to fix the devastation he caused. The animal was dead, the house destroyed. I held my son's hand tight, and we ran out of that house and kept running as fast as we could. All we had were the clothes on our back. Everything we had accumulated, had worked so hard for, gone. In the distance, I could hear my husband calling to me: "I love you. Don't leave. Come back. I hate you. I'll kill you."

Harming pets is a warning sign of escalating violence. Yet survivors often stay in the relationship out of concern for pets, and most domestic violence crisis centers do not have the capacity to provide shelter for pets. Organizations such as Red Rover and Allie Phillips offer resources and emergency shelters for humans and pets fleeing domestic violence. In some states, including here in Massachusetts, survivors can include protection for their pets when applying for a restraining order.

I couldn't dial a number, but then my boss's phone number popped into my head. I called her, and she came and quickly grabbed us up and hid us in the rectory until we could find another place to go. Her words still resonate in my head: "Selma, you need to get out of here. He is going to kill you." I knew we would never go back. To this day I don't even know how I was able to put one foot in front of the other. To run with only the clothes on your back. To see and feel and hear the pain of your child. To know you must survive.

It is a blur yet so clear, a pain that runs so very deep that I fear it will never go away. It is guilt for my child losing his dad. He deserved a father, but I deserved to be treated with respect. We were running for good this time. I knew I would never go back.

Becca: I didn't know I would leave until he beat me up over twenty dollars. TWENTY DOLLARS. Money was the "sticking" point, the object of his desire, the object of his rage, the object of my pain.

We were living on the street, then we were living on welfare. After I got my apartment, I supported the three of us on $491.00 a month. That dollar amount will always be ingrained in my memory. Welfare was *not* my preferred choice of lifestyle, but at that point I had no choice. I had worked since I was 14. I held down three jobs in high school so I could pay "rent" to family, and so I could save up for college. No one from my family would help me with college.

Welfare was the only choice I had. He was an abusive alcoholic, incapable of work. And I would never, not for any dollar amount, leave him alone with my daughter.

So I stayed, and bought diapers, baby wipes, and food, along with cigarettes and bottom-shelf vodka for him.

I didn't make a plan to leave. I never did. He was all I had, which wasn't much of anything.

I stayed, and he drank.

I stayed, and he beat me.

I stayed, and he raped me.

Finally, the night he beat me up over my last twenty dollars, I left. I needed diapers. He needed vodka. He had his priorities. I stuck to mine . . . and paid dearly. It was the first time I told him "no." He beat me. He raped me. My daughter was in the back bedroom, fast asleep. When he left the room to go to the bathroom, I saw my opportunity and ran for help. I ran out the front door, he ran out the back. The police came. The next day, they returned that twenty dollars to me in a plastic evidence bag.

Starting to take control can often lead to escalation of violence. In *Why Does He Do That?*, Lundy Bancroft explains: "When [the abuser] feels a partner starting to get stronger, beginning to think for herself more, slipping out from under domination, abusers move to their endgame." Common tactics include threats, apologies, and manipulation. The main goal of these escalating tactics is to regain control.

Donna-Marie: My therapist told me something I will never forget. She stated that the relationship I had with my abuser was like the relationship I had with my mother as a child. For the first time in my life, I realized that what I had been trying to run away from was smacking me right in the middle of my face again. At that point, I knew I had to leave the relationship.

But leaving didn't break my cycle, because I ended up in another abusive relationship. Day after day another little piece of me was gone. And then there was nothing left of me, "Donna-Marie."

So, again I left. I knew that to heal from my past, I had to go back to Boston, where it all started, and face my worst fears. I packed up my Nissan Quest and my daughter, and I hit the road. We had no idea where we were going to end up. We lived in a car, we lived with my biological mother, we lived on the Cape . . . we lived all over Massachusetts. We house-hopped and couch-surfed for nine months.

Olive: How many times did I leave? It was a major process. Thinking about leaving? Which time? Somebody told me that it takes an average of seven attempts to leave before someone is successful.

One day my neighbor saw my abuser trip me in the road. She started helping me then. I finally moved. But it didn't end there. He stalked me. His car would just appear out of nowhere. He was trying to intimidate me. He'd speed up and stop just short of my bumper. I had no idea that he'd put a GPS system in my car to track me. He tracked me via OnStar. He'd call the OnStar line to say he was worried about me and ask where I was.

> **Abusers have become savvy about using multiple forms of technology to track survivors. A car's GPS tracking system, location services on smart phones, and a survivor's computer, cell phone, iPad, and email all present opportunities for an abuser to monitor the survivor's correspondence, usage, and whereabouts.**
>
> **See Appendix for information on technology safety.**

Everywhere I go, even now, I glance in my rearview mirror to make sure he's not following me. I paid so much attention to his ways that I forgot about me. I was so completely inside his head that I could anticipate his every move. But I lost myself. I didn't know myself any more.

The very last time I was with him there was a major incident. I had a job caring for a child from 9:00 at night to 7:00 in the morning. He would drop me off at work in the evening with my baby daughter in the car. One night he was particularly terrible. He sped the car over the bridge and threatened me. All I could do was keep my eyes on my daughter.

After I left him, he was supposed to pay child support. But he didn't. Every time I asked him for it, the cycle started all over again. I was a single mom with three kids. Somehow I made it without him.

Cecilia: The reason I finally left my second abuser for good? I was pregnant with my son, and my abuser he elbowed me hard and gave me a sharp pain in my stomach. I got up and pushed him. He pushed back and slapped me. My daughter came running and said, "Mommy, this is what my daddy did to you." She was crying. I knew then I had to leave.

There was a pay phone in the apartment complex, and I called for help. The woman on the other end of the line asked me if I was safe to talk and if there was a number she could reach me. I was so afraid and kept looking up and down the street to see if he was coming. I just wanted to get away. She told me how to get to the police station in Waltham.

I took my daughter and went to the police station. My abuser had grabbed my other daughter, the daughter that he had fathered, away from me. The police officer saw I had scratches and bruises and went and arrested him. My daughter saw her father arrested. That was so hard. It was real. That was when I knew it was over. The police officers brought my other daughter to me and helped us. They took us to the hospital and then to a local shelter.

When I went to the hospital, a doctor at Children's Hospital noticed the bruises on my body. He must have called someone, because a man met me in his office and told me that I had to do something about the abuse or my kids would be taken away. I knew he was serious. I found the toll-free number for the Massachusetts Safelink hotline (1-877-785-2020) on the door of the hospital bathroom. It took me a while to make the phone call. I was afraid he would be listening or that they weren't going to help. I didn't really believe the help was real. The first time I called the hotline, I was so scared that I hung up. I called again and they walked me through the process. I was so scared someone would come to my house, so scared that *he* would know I had said something.

My daughter is the one who gave me the strength to leave. If it wasn't for her crying eyes, I don't think I ever would have left. She woke me up. We never went back.

Heidi Bluming, a Second Step intern working on her master's degree in social work at Boston College, leads a group exercise and encourages each woman to write her own positive ending to this sentence: "Because I left . . ."

- Because I left, I can be myself.

- Because I left, I got a college degree.

- Because I left, I can parent my daughter effectively.

- Because I left, I am learning to love myself.

- Because I left, I believe in my future.

- Because I left, I am empowered for greatness.

Shout It from The Mountaintops

"I was convinced that I could do this on my own."
— Donna-Marie

"Suddenly, there was no more silence. Suddenly, everyone knew."
— Olive

Becca arrives a little late to the meeting, and it is clear that she is upset. With a bit of prodding, the group learns that Becca is dismayed because her ten-year-old daughter doesn't have many friends and is in a school that Becca feels is not providing the programs and academics best suited for her. Becca breaks down in tears, and the group quickly rallies around her and offers suggestions and encouragement. Allison says that her nine-year-old son is transferring to a special program in another school, and she encourages Becca to continue to advocate hard for her daughter.

The group checks in . . .

The topic for the evening is how each woman first spoke out and shared the news that she was being abused.

Donna-Marie: I finally reached out and called a friend. I told her how unhappy I was with my life, how I wanted better for my daughter and for myself. She reminded me of a friend of ours who worked for The Second Step. I told her that I didn't need that kind of help. I was convinced that I could do this on my own. But when I finally got tired of the house hopping and couch surfing, I reached out to The Second Step.

Raquel was my case manager, and the first time we connected we talked just a little. She asked about basketball and my daughter, and I began to open up just a little bit.

I confessed that I didn't know where we would sleep or how we would eat, and Raquel suggested I meet with her. I was still on the fence, because life had already taught me that I couldn't trust anyone.

After our initial meeting, Raquel called at least once a week to check on us. She helped me to see that I needed help, but in my head I knew that I wouldn't need much, because I still believed I had to get myself out of my own mess.

My daughter and I finally found a two-bedroom apartment I could afford. We had no beds, no cookware, just our lovable smiles and each other.

Raquel checked in to see what we still needed for the apartment. I told her we had only one queen-size air mattress to sleep on. When she offered to help me get a bed, I said, "Sure." But I didn't believe she'd do anything about it.

I was shocked when she called me a week later and said that a bed would be delivered to my apartment the next day. My eyes teared up. I couldn't believe that someone who barely knew me would go to such lengths to get a proper bed for me and my daughter.

As promised, the bed arrived the next day. I was overwhelmed. I called Raquel and thanked her a million times.

At this point, I was talking with Raquel every week, but now the conversations were a little bit more personal and detailed about my life and what I had been through. I began to trust her.

Olive: My sisters knew about the abuse but just wanted me to leave the guy. I isolated them from him and wouldn't invite them to the house. There was a lady from Haiti who came to the house every morning at 7:00 to help me with the kids. I'd take half of my paycheck and give it to her every week so I could work and go to school. After a while she caught on to the abuse that was happening. Even though I don't speak Creole and she didn't speak English, we still managed to communicate.

Then, on one of my regular Saturday trips to the hair salon, I finally told someone. This was a person I never thought I would tell. Suddenly, there was no more silence. Suddenly, everyone knew. "He is beating her," the beautician said. And she said it loudly. The drama started unfolding. It was now in the open, and I was scared.

She wasted no time. She put me in her car and drove me to the police station. I did not want to go in but they persuaded me to file a report. Afterward, this woman came home with me and stayed for the weekend. She brought a baseball bat to protect me.

But no one could really protect me. Eventually my abuser came back, and, when he did, he slammed down four bookcases, and all the books fell all around my little baby. I remember my son just looking at me; thankfully, he wasn't hurt physically. My abuser pounded me to a pulp that day. It was one of the worst beatings I've ever gotten. I called 911; he pulled the phone out of the wall. The police still came and took him to jail. It was that day that I realized how complicated it all was.

I felt so guilty. I felt I had hurt him, had done something to him. So even after the reporting and the arrest, in between, I felt like I had done something wrong to him. I took him back. I even wrote a letter to the judge before the trial, offering excuses for what he'd done. The judge called me to the stand to make sure I meant what I had written.

But the judge didn't let him out of jail. I used to go and visit him with my mother-in-law. At first, I thought his mother was so kind and spiritual. But she was evil.

She was living with me at the time. She tried to make me feel remorse for putting him in jail. She was a voodoo priestess, and she put me in a psychological hold. She would toss water in each corner of my house. I kept finding dried flowers on my dresser. I was scared. I was pretty sure she had already done some spells to hurt me. She was very controlling. In hindsight, I can see that his behavior was a lot like hers.

> Sometimes culture can surface as another method of power and control. Survivors may end up feeling more isolated and stuck as a result of family members who enable abusive behavior through calling and harassing the survivor. In *The Power To Break Free*, Anisha Durve identifies some of the ways in which culture can play a part—by emphasizing the survival of the family unit over the needs of the individual, by reinforcing themes of self sacrifice and surrender as an expectation of all wives, and through the cultural taboo of divorce.

Selma: I was a bright and pretty young woman before I met him, and all in life awaited me. Once the abuse started, I should have shouted it from the mountains until someone listened. Never in my wildest dreams could I have imagined what would be dealt to me and what would become of my life as a result of my relationship with him. His actions have put my life in jeopardy and put my freedom at risk—a situation I am still dealing with today. Trust me: run, run, and don't look back. It doesn't and won't ever get better. Please spare yourself the pain, hurt, and barriers I must now deal with.

I always thought it was me somehow. What could I do differently to make it better? Was I not pretty enough? Smart enough? What was it? It took me a long time to feel I was not alone and that others, sad as the fact is, are out there. There are more of us than I want to acknowledge. But I now know that it was a process that he inflicted on me, that it wasn't my doing, and that I wasn't guilty of anything more than just trying to love someone. Search for that ray of hope. Find your own Second Step. It's out there for you. Find your sisters. We are here, waiting for you.

> **Lisa Aaronson Fontes, author of *Invisible Chains*, describes how survivors often blame themselves for the abuse they have endured— they become brainwashed and begin to accept their partner's view that it is their fault.**

Carole: You have an amazing attitude, despite the bad stuff and the abuse.

Selma: Life is short. None of us walk this journey untarnished. We all make our mistakes and learn. I've gotten to the point in my life that it's no longer about judging anybody, just learning to accept others for who they are. And I'm talking about all walks of life. I'm trying to take one step forward at a time, trying to become a better person. To figure out the things that are important to me. So, in a way it's selfish, but in another way it's accepting and forgiving.

Carole: That's remarkable. To have gone through what you've gone through and still see the positive. You have an amazing capacity for loving and forgiving.

Sherry: The word "selfish" has such negative connotations. What you're really doing is creating your sense of self. In that sense, selfish is a really good thing.

Selma: Someone recently said to me: "This lifetime is nothing more than a blink of an eye." Can you even imagine what eternity is? Why not take that blink of an eye and make it all that you can?

Olive: Things changed when I found The Second Step. My Second Step mentor and I met regularly. It was the first time I ever went out for coffee. She did a lot with me. I'd forgotten that people did this, I'd forgotten about girl time. She'd bring me treats, or call me and bring the kids to Burger King and to the park, just to give me some time alone.

On the day my daughter was born, my mentor came to the hospital with me., gowned up, and was at my side the whole time. She was such a cheerleader for me. When I delivered my daughter, they gave her to my mentor before bringing her to me. That's how close we were. I think I would have died without her. My abuser didn't know about her. I kept her top secret.

At The Second Step, we come in feeling like victims. Now we don't feel like victims any more. I have learned a lot here. I finally see what my true strengths are. So many people believed in me when I didn't believe in myself. The amount of resources available made it possible for me to take care of myself. I've learned how to gather resources for my family and for myself.

It Ain't Over Yet

"One of us may die today, but it's not going to be me."
— Olive

"Every survivor is the expert on her abuser."
— Carole

As we discussed earlier in the book, leaving is the most dangerous time. Even when the relationship is over, often the survivor must have contact with the abuser, who frequently continues to pose a threat. Because the abuser may continue to stalk the survivor long after the relationship has ended, safety planning continues to be vitally important.

The group checks in . . .

Tonight, the women discuss the ongoing need to be hyper-vigilant about their safety, even after they have left their abusers.

Becca: I feel like they're always ten steps ahead of us. I used to keep my hair in a bun, so he couldn't grab it. Even when you try to move on, they leave an imprint on your life. You want to move on, but you're like…what if …?

Carole: There are some tactics of abuse, such as strangulation, that can elevate to a lethal level. Dr. Judith Campbell did a national study of risk factors for "femicide" (female homicide) and based on her research findings created a dangerousness assessment tool. It was developed a while ago, but it continues to be relevant and useful today.

Olive: I had a big fight with my ex just the other day. He usually takes the kids on Saturdays so I can go to class. He will often drive me. But he is always late, and on this day I

No More Secrets

was determined to get to class on time, so I decided to drive myself. But just as I was pulling out of my driveway, he pulled in behind me, blocking me. We immediately started to fight. He said he wouldn't drive me until my daughter was ready. I insisted he drive me to class first and then come back and get my daughter. He finally relented, but he was angry.

On the drive to school, I could feel his anger escalating, and he started to try to control me. I was texting my daughter, and he demanded that I stop. *He* was the one driving, not me. But he wanted my undivided attention. When I didn't stop texting, he tried to yank the phone away from me and then started radically swerving the car. I told him I was going to call 9-1-1.

He pulled into a residential area and stopped the car, and my brain kicked into overdrive, running through all the coping tools I'd learned: There are people here, families walking about, people who will help me.

I saw that old familiar monster come up in his eyes. Usually I look away — anything not to have to look into those eyes.

"Do you know you are this close to dying?" he hissed at me.

I lifted my head and looked straight into his eyes.

"One of us may die today," I said, "But it's not going to be me."

I got out of the car, knowing he would come after me. I knew what to do. I made sure that my window was rolled up all the way, and I pushed down the button so the door would lock behind me. As I knew he would, he got out and chased me around the car. I jumped in to the driver's seat, slammed and locked the door, and roared off. He chased the car as long as he could and then walked the two miles to my class. He had the nerve to come in and ask me for the car keys!

I am done with this. I know now I can never again be alone with him. I can't keep asking him for rides or for rides for my kids. I can see he's getting desperate.

The medicine I am now taking seems to be making a big difference. I feel calmer, more like myself, and more in control. Our court case is still unresolved, the child support is still unresolved, but I know I can do just fine on my own.

Cecilia: Child support is not worth it. It's too stressful, the price is too high. It's too hard to have him in my life, in my house. It's not easy doing it on my own, but it's better than trying to do it with him.

I worked fourteen hours today. I'm tired, but I'm strong. I let him go so I can be free. He takes too much of my energy.

Becca: Abusers can bring us down so much. But I always tell everyone "I'm fine."

Donna-Marie: Our favorite words: "I'm fine."

Olive: He comes to the house to get my kids. One day I was freaking out, because my car keys were gone. It turns out he'd hidden them. He wants me to think I'm losing my mind. I'm not living my life fully. It's hard. He's the father to my children. He has to have access. I'll never be released. It's exhausting.

Day by day, just when I think things are getting better, he keeps creeping in. He has my life chained. I needed passports and permission from him to take my kids to travel for my grandmother's funeral. I had to give him flight information and phone numbers or he would have had me arrested for running away with our kids.

Donna-Marie: It doesn't matter how much therapy you go through. I'm always looking to see if my abuser is there. After we split up, she would continue to call me on my house phone or cell phone, asking: "What bitch is in your house?" and threatening to drive by and throw a brick through the window. "Don't let me catch you on the sheets because I'mma fuck you up," she'd say. I would stay awake all night long worrying that she'd come by. I made a point to avoid places where she might be, so as not to run into her.

Olive: It ties up your dating life forever. You can't be free. He's there, he's going to know. Why take the chance? I find a way to sabotage any new relationship even if I'm having the nicest conversations.

Donna-Marie: It's like retraining your brain. If you had a bad childhood, it's hard to picture normalcy. You're trained to always expect the worst.

Carole: If you had one magic wish, what would it be? What would you do to put him in his place and move on?

Olive: I'd turn him into a freakin' toad so I could step on him. Or I'd make him wear a book, tattoo it onto him: "This is me, what I'm like, what everyone should be scared of."

Becca: I wish he would get help. I was so young, such a fixer. If I knew he were in a better place, not hurting other women, I could move on . . . I don't have a revenge fantasy . . . but . . . I would light a firecracker, stick it up his ass, and let it go.

Olive: Me of all people. I'm open-hearted and kind. But then, 10, 15, 20 times, you're telling me the same thing. Go to hell!

Donna-Marie: I just don't want to ever see her again. I don't want her to know anything about me.

Olive: As long as I live in this town, he's going to find me. I just moved, and he moved around the corner from me! It's a new home, a new beginning for me. But he's starting to pick the kids up everyday and come inside the house with them. I can't sleep; I've started cleaning non-stop again. I can't stop.

Carole: It's time to reset the boundaries. He's pushing you again. This is another reminder that it's important to continue planning for your safety. You have to stay one step ahead of him. You know him best. Every survivor is the expert on her abuser.

There are many resources available to help survivors, whether they are in a relationship or have left the relationship. See the Appendix for safety planning and resources.

Seeking Shelter

"There were a lot of rules and a lot of people.
I felt like an octopus, pulled first one way and then another."
—Cecilia

Before this meeting begins in earnest, the women start to talk about the issue of "belonging." Allison says that, at one point, she saw Donna-Marie crying and felt like Donna-Marie was the one who belonged in the group, not her. Donna-Marie confessed, in turn, that she felt some of the people in the group had progressed so far beyond their abusive relationships that she was the one who didn't belong. And Selma confessed that, when she first learned that Allison had been in her abusive relationship a mere three months, she thought to herself, "That's not domestic violence," not realizing the long history of abusive family dynamics that Allison had endured. Over time, she has come to understand that even one day in an abusive relationship is one day too many.

Becca summed up the feelings of the entire group when she said that it is the very difference of experiences and variations in the levels of healing that lends the richness and strength to the group as a whole. "We all wind up benefitting from one another's experiences," she says.

The group checks in . . .

The discussion topic for the evening, emergency shelters and transitional living, gets a mixed reaction from the group. While each woman expresses appreciation for the help and support she received, a few confess that the help came with an emotional cost. It can be stressful suddenly to find oneself living with strangers and having to adhere to house rules that can seem restrictive. But for survivors who don't have friends or families who can take them in, emergency shelter and transitional housing are necessary waypoints on the road to a safe and independent life.

The women share their tips and coping skills for navigating shelter and transitional housing life:

1. Create a goal plan.

2. Be respectful of others' space and time.

3. Work with a good, objective therapist, who is trained in domestic violence.

4. Pray.

5. Spend time with friends outside of the shelter.

6. Remember that emergency housing is a place to be safe and just a brief step in building your new life. Do not be discouraged by the rules, even though at times they can seem dehumanizing. Just do the chores and maintain the curfew. Keep reminding yourself that you are safe and free of abuse.

7. Breathe.

8. Do not spend all of your time in the shelter environment. Keep yourself busy with employment, school, or pursuing goals for life after the shelter. Too much time in the shelter without an outlet can make you depressed, complacent, and sap your motivation to work toward goal plans.

9. Do not rely on the shelter staff to fix problems for you. Part of being a head of a household is learning to be resourceful and how to advocate for yourself.

10. Speak up and ask about food and clothing and whatever else you need. Shelters all receive donations and funding, but in most cases you will need to advocate for yourself and ask for what you need. If one person doesn't offer help, then go to another. Housemates can be a great source of information.

11. A little tolerance goes a long way. Not everyone will clean the way you want things cleaned. Not everyone will have the same morals or values as you. Just because you live a certain way doesn't mean everyone else has to live that way also. We are all cut from different cloth.

12. Don't "sweat the small stuff."

13. Concentrate on where you are going, not where you came from.

14. Remember that this living situation is transitional and temporary.

Allison: I was apprehensive about moving into transitional housing because of the preconceived notions I had about shelter life. I grew up in a strict Christian home, and my family believed that shelters were for drug addicts, alcoholics, or people with no hope in life. The Second Step removed every negative thought I had about shelter life. I was amazed at how beautiful, clean, and organized my new home was.

The Second Step staff encouraged me to seek therapy in order to heal from my past. I had some reservations about this. There's a real stigma about therapy in the black community. We think it's only white people who have issues! Now I know that could not be further from the truth. Therapy has allowed me to work out the issues I've had in my life. Now I'm encouraging all people from every walk of life, including black folks, to seek counseling.

During one of my meetings with my case manger, I expressed interest in returning to school. I only had a high school diploma, so my employment options were limited to working in factories and fast food restaurants. This didn't provide the income I needed to raise three children as a single parent.

But college did not feel realistic to me. I came from a home where college was not even an option; it was straight to work right after high school. The Second Step made the idea of college not only realistic, but they helped to make it happen. With encouragement from my case manager I enrolled in a community college. This was a huge accomplishment for me, especially given that both of my parents were elementary school and middle school dropouts.

Cecilia: I knew I had to get to a safe place for my kids. I was pregnant with my son and I had two daughters. I went to a shelter. I had never been in one before. I was very scared, and at first it was hard for me to trust anyone. The woman who helped me was very kind. The shelter had a three-month limit, but they let me stay a little longer. But when I went into the hospital to have my son, I had to temporarily sign my kids over to the Department of Social Services because there was no one to look after them for me.

After I had my baby, I left the emergency shelter and went to live at The Second Step. There were a lot of rules and a lot of people. I felt like an octopus, pulled first one way and then the other. But The Second Step gave my family a lot. For starters, they gave me two rooms — one for my older girls and the other for my baby and me. It was so nice to have that space and to be able to settle in. My older daughter went to school, and my younger daughter was enrolled in the Head Start program. It was the first time I could be alone with my baby. I remember feeling such joy over something as simple as making peanut butter cookies. I felt like I was home.

The Second Step helped me to find permanent housing and helped me get settled. Now, after 10 years, I still feel safe. I know that someone is there for me. I don't feel alone. When I listen to the women in the Narrative Healing Group now, I feel like I can come closer to who I want to be. I'm starting to talk. We have something in common. I'm learning from them.

Selma: When I lived in transitional housing, it was dictated to me that I had to apply for food stamps and housing. Many of the meetings I was mandated to attend were degrading. One was a coloring session. I know it was meant to be therapeutic, but I am in my 40s. Many staff members were great, but there were others that were borderline abusive and controlling. It was almost as if they found pleasure in belittling us.

Every time I was made to feel "less than," I wanted to run back to my abuser. But each time I stopped myself and worked through it. I knew that one day soon I would have a safe, happy home for my son and myself.

I never applied for permanent housing while in transitional housing and later regretted this decision. It really doesn't hurt to apply, and it speeds up the process. It is possible to work and generate a good living while in housing. You don't need to accept it, but it is good to have if you need it. I wish I had known how much of a journey my healing was going to take. I just thought I needed to work and get a place to live and we would be fine. Then the real life issues of post-traumatic stress disorder and depression taught me differently. My healing is still ongoing at this stage.

In general, the women I lived with were great. In many ways we were like family—caring for each other and all of our children. Occasionally a bad apple comes into the mix. Don't let this change your vision or alter your path.

When things get hard, look into your little one's eyes. They really did hear the yelling; they really did feel and see the abuse. Is this the life you want for them? If you don't have children, then look in the mirror. You really do deserve to live a life without abuse. No one should have to live with domestic violence. The unknown is so scary. Taking the first step is hard, but it will pay off each and every day. Each step you take gets you closer. Don't give up.

Becca: The homeless shelter system in Boston was not very helpful in keeping me safe. I don't think I trusted any caseworker enough to share the abuse that I was dealing with.

One shelter had a bed lottery. You had to be there by 3:00 p.m. and, if you didn't happen to win the lottery, you were out. You had to wait outside for a bed to become available. Another shelter separated men and women, but it was still a toss-up whether you would get a bed there.

Shelter staff would offer substance abuse and mental health assistance, but I kept falling through the cracks because I was pregnant and experiencing domestic violence.

The requirements of the transitional living shelter were not conducive to healing from trauma. For me, it wasn't a safe place to just be and sleep and heal.

Donna-Marie: I didn't even know shelters were an option. I stayed with friends. Once I got my own apartment, I contacted The Second Step.

Amber: Leaving wasn't the hard part. It's surviving that's a mess. I didn't know who I was anymore. I couldn't tell you my favorite things to eat. You're not who you started out to be, and you're not who he made you. You're something in between. I used to tell the people running the shelters: I was married for 20 years. It took that long to make me this way, please don't throw me out in 30 days.

Caring For Your Cubs

"I realized that I was preparing a soldier, not raising a child."
— Allison

"I think we put blinders on regarding our children."
— Selma

The women are in high spirits this evening. They had been out to a karaoke bar earlier in the week and are still basking in the glow of the experience. There is much good-natured ribbing and commentary about everyone's singing abilities. Once the joking settles down, the group turns its attention to the question at hand: How to address the challenges of raising children in a household shadowed by domestic violence, especially in light of recent studies showing that even very young children are affected.

It turns out to be a pivotal night for the group. Whereas Sherry and Carole typically facilitate the discussion and guide the women, offering gentle nudges of support and counsel, on this night they are mostly silent. The women themselves keep the conversation moving and are quick to offer suggestions, perspective, and tough love whenever they deem it necessary. Before our very eyes the group members have become its leaders.

The group checks in . . .

Becca: My abuser's control over me was absolute. He somehow convinced me to name my daughter "Envy." For years, "Envy" was her official first name. His rationale was that it was "edgy, and so cool."

Abuse takes many forms, and Envy's name was like a shadow over my life. He was out of our lives physically, but his presence made itself known every time I had to use her official name on a school document or medical record. That name gave him continued ownership of her and kept him in our lives in such an insidious way.

A name is so powerful; it's at the core of our beings. I couldn't imagine Envy having to go through life with that name. When she was eleven, I began the process of having her name changed officially to Kayla. She wrote a note to the judge saying that she got embarrassed every time the teachers called her "Envy." The judge actually used some of her language in the new birth certificate, which states that her former name is "inappropriate and embarrassing."

Selma: I wish someone had made me see what my son was going through. I wish they had taken me by the shoulders and given me a good shake, to wake me up and make me see.

Cecilia: Me, too. If I had to do it again, I'd leave earlier. I worry that I did a lot of damage by staying.

Selma: I thought I was doing the right thing by staying, by providing my young son with a father figure and a complete family unit.

Sherry: How do you know your son was hurt by what he witnessed?

Selma: Even now, he'll hear a noise and will jump and say, "That sounds like when dad raped you."

It's so hard to hear that from my child. I would die for him. Why I was in such denial during that time is beyond my understanding. Why didn't I scream during the rapes? But I wanted my son to love his dad. Plus, I was alone, alienated.

Carole: You have a fantasy about the relationship being normal and healthy . . . when bad stuff happens you keep thinking that this just a temporary blip on the screen and not part of your "normal" relationship.

Selma: I must have been sick not to realize that it's never OK to be abused. I was so broken. I succumbed to his world.

Donna-Marie: I wouldn't say you were sick. That had become your new normal.

Olive: My kids haven't said too much about what they experienced. Even though they experienced abuse from the womb. The abuse started when I was four months pregnant. He used to sit on my legs so I couldn't move, and would talk and talk and talk at me. My baby was hearing this before he was even born.

My kids know he's a complete jerk. They're 11- and 13-years-old now, and he can't fool them.

Somehow, I was able to teach them my values. I think one day they'll acknowledge that he hit me. I know they know, and one day they'll ask me about it. When they do, we'll have an honest conversation.

> According to Betsy McAlister Groves, licensed clinical social worker and founding director of Boston Medical Center's Child Witness to Violence Project, domestic violence is "a particularly toxic form of trauma for children." Children experiencing domestic violence in the home learn early on that no place is safe, adults are vulnerable, and adults cannot protect them. Their fear often leads to aggression. Groves' 2012 project studying the impact of domestic violence on children revealed that 85% of children witnessing domestic violence had moderate or severe symptoms of post-traumatic stress disorder.

Cecilia: My daughter saw a lot of violence, and now at age 23 she's abusive towards me.

Carole: It's learned behavior.

Cecilia: My little ones are not abusive at all. But my older daughter is. She said to me: "You're nothing but a punching bag." One time when she was hitting me, I turned around to look at her and saw this horrible face. It was her father's face.

She has a lot of issues herself. She has problems with men and can't hold down a job. She's back living with me now and going to school part-time.

Part of me didn't want her to come back home. But she's my daughter. I had to help her. But even though I tried to lay down some ground rules this time, in less than three months we were back to the same old abusive routine.

Olive: You have to call her on it. She's being abusive.

Cecilia: She's like her father. He would hit me and make me bleed and then say, "Look what you made me do. Go clean yourself up."

Sherry: How is it for the younger kids seeing this abuse?

Cecilia: My son is 11-years-old. He's confused. He loves me but he loves his older sister, too.

Selma: Do you worry that your younger children will become abusive after witnessing her behavior? Because we do have choices. My older son came back, and I laid down the ground rules and explained that there would be consequences if he broke them. The night he came home drunk and high I told him that I loved him and that he had to leave. I told him point blank that there's no room in our household for this type of behavior. Ever.

It's so hard to say this to your child. I've paid to put him in rehab. I've done everything I can think to do to help him. But he's a grown man. Finally, I had to say, "Enough. Done. I love you. I'll pray for you. Call me." And then pushed him out the door.

I am worried about my younger son. The people we're living with are trying to get him to shut off the TV, but he needs that to help him feel safe. He sleeps with me now. My heart is really going out to him and what he's going through. The other day, he told me that once he graduates from college he is going to rent a limo, find his father, and say, "Look at me now, Dad. I am nothing like you."

Allison: I worry about my kids, too. At one point I took a step back and looked at how I was treating my kids, especially my

14-year-old daughter. I realized that I was preparing a soldier, not raising a child. I was preparing her for war because of my own experiences.

Sleeping with the TV on is not that uncommon. Many of my friends admit that they sleep with the TV on. One of them is this big six foot three, 300-pound dude and he told me his TV broke so now he can't sleep.

Selma: I think we put blinders on regarding our children. We tell ourselves that our children never see or hear anything. Our instincts tell us that, as their protector, we won't allow them to be a part of the world we're dealing with. We think we're experiencing the domestic violence all alone, but this is the furthest from the truth. If someone had shown me the implications of what my son was feeling as a result of what he witnessed, I would have left my abuser right then.

Carole: You think you're managing it all so well, but children know.

Donna-Marie: We think they don't know. And they don't always know directly. But they have bad dreams or are anxious and upset and can't express why.

Carole: Cecilia sleeping in her car, "her greenhouse," and letting her daughter stay with her dad was a way to manage an impossible situation, because she knew her daughter would actually be safer there with him.

Cecilia: The sad thing is, to this day, my daughter thinks I don't love her. She can't forgive me for leaving her.

Sherry: The awful thing is, there is no good answer. You were caught. In that moment you made the best decision you could.

Cecilia: I didn't even know there were such things as shelters. I didn't know there was a place we could go. If I had, I would not have left my daughter behind on those nights I spent in the "greenhouse."

Once we did learn about the shelters and all of us went there, that was when she needed me most. But I was so stressed out by all the rules that I couldn't care for her. I can never forgive myself for that. So now I let her argue with me and do what she wants.

Olive: Have you ever tried to explain this to her? She's a grown woman now; she might understand.

Cecilia: She's angry with me and doesn't let me in. She says I only love my other children and I don't love her.

Selma: You are an amazing mother. You can't beat yourself up about the past. The more I stop helping my kids the more it forces them to live their lives.

There is *no* room in your house for abuse. You cannot allow your younger children to see the abuse. By letting your daughter abuse you, you're saying to your kids that this behavior is okay.

Cecilia: Sometimes I wonder if it would have been better if I had just walked away and left her with her father.

Donna-Marie: She's abusive because she's witnessed that behavior and because she is so angry. Because she's your child, you're willing to take it because you feel so guilty. You're allowing your young kids to see their sister abuse you. How is that going to make them feel?

Olive: If you allow your older daughter to stay in your home and continue to abuse you, then your younger kids are at risk of becoming abusive. My oldest is 20. She ran away. She stole from me. I had her arrested several times. I did everything I could to save her. But I couldn't.

When she was seven years old, my parents took her and raised her. She didn't realize until later that I hadn't raised her. When she did, she got angry. She became a monster at age 13. She terrorized me when she came back and lived with me. She was unable to connect with me because I was still with my abuser. It created a lot of anger in her.

When you're riddled with guilt, it's so hard to get past it. I couldn't stand my child. It was so hard to connect with her when I was going through such a hard time myself.

Selma: I've met your daughter. You've done something to turn her around.

Olive: When she showed up at my door, pregnant, I used that as a way to get close to her again. I told her that I would be there for her and her child. I was able to tell her that I knew it was not the best for her that I'd let my parents raise her and that I would do everything I could to help her be with her child.

She's still rough around the edges, though. But I would bet, Cecilia, that your daughter still wants a relationship with you. But if you're not careful, your two other kids are going to turn on you.

Cecilia: I don't want to hear that.

Selma: She is a grown woman. It's your two younger children who need you. And don't you realize that a Department of Children and Families social worker could take your kids away? Imagine the damage that could do. When it comes to the welfare of our minor children, they need us. You have to look after them. That doesn't mean you don't love your older daughter.

Donna-Marie: It's tough love. Sometimes you have to love people from afar. That's what I had to do. It was the only way I could heal.

Olive: My daughter left home last week. I told her, "This is it." I told her I would help her any way I could, but that she is not living with me again.

Donna-Marie to Cecilia: What are your daughter's responsibilities at home?

Cecilia: She has none. I pay all her bills. She doesn't work.

Olive: Put your foot down.

Donna-Marie: Or better yet, put it up her ass. You are a puppet, and she is pulling your strings. You have a choice. She is a grown woman. She can go live with a roommate.

Allison: Have you heard that story about the prodigal son? He wants his wealth now, and the dad gives it to him. He lives his life and does horrible things and loses everything. He was a bum and lived on the street. But he knew his dad would always welcome him home. That's your daughter. Let her go out and live her life, but eventually she's going to come home to what's familiar. When you go out there in the world and it beats you down, you return to the comforts of home.

Cecilia: I'm afraid she's going to get hurt.

Allison: Let her get hurt. It's called life. She'll be back.

Olive: Sometimes it's better to let them fly.

Cecilia: I love my daughter, but I don't miss all the mess she used to make, intentionally. It is more peaceful when she's away. The younger kids are kind.

Allison: You can love her from afar. My mom used to say, "A hard head makes a soft behind." (From all the beatings.) When she comes back, just talk to her through the door. Ask her, "What do you want, girl?"

Selma: We're not beating up on you.

Sherry: What is it like for you to hear these things?

Cecilia: I think they don't understand.

Carole: I can tell you that I've heard this from many people here. They've been very much in your shoes. They aren't criticizing. They know how hard this is.

Cecilia: I feel like I'm being attacked. Like they're not sensitive to the problem.

Sherry: That must be making it hard for you, to feel like they don't really understand how difficult and painful this is for you.

Donna-Marie: I like that you're not quiet anymore. I like that you've found your voice. I love my new friends. And, I don't want to see my new friends back in a situation where they feel they can't help themselves. I am going to love you, regardless. But, I am going to tell you what I think. I don't want to see anybody hurting you again.

I saw your two little kids. I watched them play around outside with Olive's kids. Your kids are so innocent. That innocence only lasts until it is taken. We all had our innocence taken.

Selma: I'm telling you what I so badly wish someone had told me.

Olive: You feel so bad because you don't want to accept the truth. It's traumatizing to go to the counselor and be in the hot seat. I didn't want to sit there and listen to my daughter go at me. It was so hard to listen to the accusations. But I learned to listen and accept and apologize and correct. The counselor my daughter and I used assured me she was a neutral, non-judgmental third person. And you know what? She was.

Sherry to Cecilia: What's so wonderful is that everybody cares so much about you and wants so much for you.

Cecilia: It's taken me forever — ten years — to learn how to trust and to be able to speak up in this group.

Selma: I think the people who *didn't* speak were the ones who didn't care about me.

Cecilia: I'm too sensitive. That's not a good thing.

Donna-Marie *and* Olive: It is a good thing. You can be sensitive *and* speak your mind.

Cecilia: I do want to fix this problem with my daughter. But she spat in my face. What am I going to do? I asked her to go to church with me and she said "No." I feel like I'm this idiot that she hates so much.

Selma: You can't make people do what they're not ready to do. We can only control our own destiny.

Donna-Marie: She's still that little girl looking out the bedroom window at you hiding in the car, thinking that you left her. That's where she is stuck.

Cecilia: I want to tell her that I'm sorry that I never hugged her. My mother never hugged me. She tries to do it now, but it doesn't feel real.

Carole: You want your daughter to know that you love her. At the same time, you can't live with this household dynamic. I can make a referral for you for therapy. You can tell her simply that if she is going to live with you going forward, she will go to therapy. She will learn to be respectful, not abusive.

Sherry: What are the most important rules you would like her to follow?

Cecilia: 1: Don't touch my stuff. 2: Don't touch me — or the kids. 3: Don't be rude to me — or the kids.

> Cecilia is talking about setting boundaries with her daughter. Clear boundaries define how you want to be treated in a relationship. Materials from a coalition of Indiana University–Purdue University Fort Wayne suggest that a boundary is like "a fence in your backyard. You are the gatekeeper and get to decide who you let in and who you keep out, who you let into the whole back yard, and who you let just inside the gate." Setting boundaries can include: communicating without blaming, being honest and saying how you feel, and setting consequences and then following through on them.

Selma: Before I die, I want my kids to be grown and self-sufficient. That is my *job* as a parent. Things will start to change with your daughter once you start standing your ground. If you don't, things won't change.

Cecilia: I know what I want, but I need help to get through the mess.

Selma: If you can't live comfortably in your own house, then she has to go.

Cecilia: I don't even yell at her because I'm so worried about what the neighbors will think.

Selma: The last time my son tried to come home, I sent him back out in the world with a care package of resources, places he can go and people he can call. I now keep extra copies in the house. If he can't abide by my rules in the house, then he is not welcome in it. I will keep sending him back out in the world with that packet of resources.

I wish there were a crystal ball to show how the decisions we make will affect our children down the road. I'm stunned by how many kids in the public school system have IEPs (Individual Education Program).

Donna-Marie: I have three-, four-, and five-year-olds that I'm about to start a group for. They're either very aggressive or very quiet. They've all witnessed domestic violence.

Selma: How do you know where the aggressiveness comes from? I find it hard to differentiate my son's behavior: Is he modeling his father's behavior, or is he just a typical 13-year-old boy?

Donna-Marie: We've acknowledged the power of their dads, but we also have to acknowledge our own power. We're the ones who are with these kids every day.

Olive: When I tell my son he looks like his dad, he says, "I may look like him, but I'm nothing like him."

Donna-Marie: My daughter has been in counseling at Children's Hospital from age 11. I have to say, Children's Hospital was incredible. They put my daughter's needs first, and the counseling really helped.

Selma: Counseling only helps if it's a good match. When I went, I felt belittled.

Olive: I have some faith that things are getting better. For my business, I'm getting mandatory training from the state to recognize signs of domestic violence.

Selma: My son became my focus, my survival tool to keep going. We can talk about anything. He was my saving grace. Without him I think I would have jumped off a bridge.

Donna-Marie: My daughter was mine, too. If I didn't have her, I would have gone to a totally different place.

Selma: I spent so many years lying to my child. I feel so guilty about that now.

Carole: It was age appropriate to do that for your child.

Selma: I would do it differently now. I'd say, "Your father just stabbed me. Call 9-1-1." I'd tell the cops, "Slap the cuffs on him. We're out of here." I'm so proud that I can do that now.

Talking to and checking in with your children can be essential in helping them process the violence. It is important to listen to the child's experiences and feelings and to position yourself as the adult in the conversation. On their factsheet, which lists useful tips for talking to children about domestic violence, The National Child Traumatic Stress Network advises to "talk to your children in a way that's right for their ages. Use words that you know they understand. Be careful not to talk about adult concerns or to speak at an adult's level of understanding."

A Message To Caregivers
And Loved Ones

"If I had to do it all over again,
I would talk to my family about the abuse."

— Allison

"I wish the social workers who worked with me
had asked if I was being abused."

— Becca

Spring is in the air this evening, and the group comes together with a certain lightness of being. Maybe it's just the shedding of boots and gloves and jackets and all the layering that comes with a New England winter. Maybe it's something more.

As she typically does, Sherry has brought dinner, and the women help themselves to salad, grilled chicken, pita, hummus, and rice crackers. Sherry brings a different meal each week, and, no matter what the menu, it makes everyone feel valued, cared for, and nurtured.

Becca has brought in an extra treat: strawberries, pastry shells, and whipped cream for "make our own" strawberry shortcakes. Olive has never before tasted whipped cream, and the room goes silent watching her first figure out how to use the spray can and then have her first taste. She brings the spoon to her mouth and breaks into a broad smile. It's a sweet beginning to the evening's session.

The group checks in . . .

The past has come back to turn Selma's life upside down. She has just lost her job, but has another job interview on Friday and is optimistic. She is living at a friend's house for the moment, sharing a room with her son and the friend's dog. It is not ideal, she says, but for now it's home.

Becca and Allison have just finished their final exams. Both will continue to take classes over the summer but are pleased to have a few weeks off from their studies.

The topic for the evening is what the women wish they had told their families and friends, and how they wish they had helped. We start with a writing exercise, and some of the women choose to write as though they are writing directly to their loved ones. Following the exercise, the women begin to share.

Selma: You treated me like I was a grown up and let me make my own decisions. I can see that you were trying to be respectful, but when you saw the changes in me, that I wasn't coming around to visit as much, I wish you had come in full force. I wish you had never given up on me.

When you suspected I was in trouble, I wish you had come to me and pulled me in and not given up until you received honest answers. I wish you had not allowed me to become isolated. I wish you had seen through the silence. I wish you had realized that, even though I was a grown woman, I still needed you. I wish you had held me even as I pushed you away. I wish you never let me leave. I wish I knew what to say. I wish you had held my hand. I wish you had provided me the security of knowing I could always go home if I needed to. I wish you had never let him take me away from you. I wish you had realized how much I needed you!

Donna-Marie: When you suspected I was in trouble, I wish you had stood up for me. I wish you had stepped in and grabbed my abuser's arm. I wish you would have wiped my tears and told me that it would be all right. I wish you could have saved me, taken me away so that no one could hurt me. I wish you had placed yourself in my shoes just once and felt the pain I endured. I wish you could have looked into my heart, my eyes, my mind and seen that I was being hurt, being damaged, being used. I wish that instead of turning your back and looking the other way, you acknowledged that something was happening. I wish you had realized that "this" would make it hard for me to trust, to believe in happy endings. I wish you had understood the life-long impact this would have on my life and on my child's life.

But, I wish you *didn't* tell me that everything was going to be okay. I wish you didn't say that sometimes a woman has to endure things that are not nice. I wish you didn't tell me to be more of a woman and to take it. I wish you didn't look at my bruises and tell me to wash up and that I'd be okay. I wish you had listened with your heart and not with your eyes. I wish you had comforted me, hugged me, let me lay my head on your shoulders and cry until I felt better. I wish you had seen the fear in my eyes every time you came over. I wish that when you turned your back, you had eyes in the back of your head. I wish you would have asked, talked, viewed, interpreted, and seen the signs. I wish you would have just loved me enough to *help,* even if you weren't sure how.

> Family members who are well intentioned and want to support the survivor may inadvertently support the power and control dynamic through excusing abusive behavior, degrading and insulting the victim for not leaving sooner or getting more help, not taking the abuse seriously, or judging the survivor for going back to the abuser.

Allison: I alienated myself from my family. They learned about my relationship through gossip they heard in the streets. I completely shut out my sister, and, for that reason, when my abuser called her looking for me, she gave him my phone number. If I had to do it all over again, I would talk to my family about my abuse. They would know why I wasn't okay. It hurts when your family has to hear about your abuse through strangers. I have learned that family is there for you when friends have walked away.

Becca: When my family suspected I was in trouble, I wish they had tried to understand fully where I was in my life, and moved beyond condemnation and judgment. I wish bystanders on the street observed my vulnerability—pregnant, abused, homeless—and asked me about it . . . and really cared about the answer. Did they think I was a lost cause?

I wish the people on the street who saw me pregnant hadn't yelled, "DCF (Department of Children and Families) should come and take that baby." I wish the social workers who worked with me had asked if I was being abused. I wish my brother hadn't said, "Get rid of him." I wish the folks that were around me recognized why I didn't show up for church, why I had to lie and lie and lie for him. I wish they had asked me. I wish I could have told them. I wish the woman on the street who bought me dinner had known how scared and in danger I really was. I wish I had told her. I wish the police officers who brought me to the train station understood how vulnerable I was and offered me more help than they did. I wish that the shelter recognized the abuse I was experiencing and didn't punish me for it. I wish the community helped me more after I was beaten up. I wish I didn't have to take the bus to the courthouse, with my 23-month-old daughter in tow, when I was in so much physical pain. I wish I could have told all of them. And I wish I could have trusted that they would help.

Olive: I wish my family and friends had been more persistent. If my sisters had tried to intervene, I probably would have told them to go to hell. But they should have kept coming back. Now I look back and think, why didn't they shoot him? Why didn't they protect me? Why did they turn their back on me? I created so much isolation around me, not even the priest could have broken through.

I wish my sisters had done then more of what they are doing now. They tell me they love me. They speak up for me.

> It's important to not place shame or blame on the survivor. It's also important to remember that you can't "rescue" your friend or family member. Family and friends can best support survivors in a few key ways: nonjudgmental listening; being proactive about offering specific help, such as childcare, meal preparation, and transportation; and connecting the survivor with domestic violence resources.

Allison: Could it be they didn't get involved because they knew you were going to go back to him? Knowing your sisters, I see that they want the best for you. But if they had gotten involved, then their husbands would have been involved also.

Olive: I didn't want that drama.

Becca: My high school English teacher tried to help me. She would read my poetry and essays, and she knew something was amiss at the house. I'd been bounced through three houses by the time I reached high school. The only thing she could do was talk to my family about it. She really tried to reach out. But it didn't work. I tried to tell her that my family was crazy but she didn't listen. I think she wanted so badly to help . . . I was doing well academically, she believed in me. I think she was in denial about how bad my family was. She wanted better for me, and I knew it, but she couldn't make it happen.

Sherry: She didn't know what to do. It's the dilemma of being a bystander, where people want to help but don't know how.

> Regina Yau, founder of the Pixel Project to end violence against women via social media and other technologies, says, bystanders can support the survivor by finding a way to safely intervene when witnessing a violent incident: bystanders should call the police, take precautions to keep themselves safe, and privately show support for the survivor and offer her information on local resources. Also, in our communities, we can prevent further systemic harm by voicing discomfort with comments that enable rape culture and abusive behavior.

Becca: But she did help. She challenged me to read books and write essays above and beyond the class workload. She showed she cared in different ways, which was nice. But I only had her for a couple of years. After that, the only person who really helped me was a fellow churchgoer who offered me the use of her car—an old 1989 Buick Skylark. Then there really was nobody until The Second Step.

Allison: I had a life-changing moment with someone in authority more than twenty years ago. I ran into a high school classmate at a local restaurant owned by my friend's father. The restaurant was in a drug-infested neighborhood, overrun with pimps and prostitutes. The man I was with at the time was a self-proclaimed gangsta/pimp/lowlife, call him what you will.

On this particular morning, I went into the restaurant and started chatting with my classmate. Her father approached and asked who I was and if I was "working the street." I replied, "No sir." He then said something to me that no one had ever said before. He told me he had encountered many people in this town and didn't see much good in many of them. But he could tell that I didn't belong there. He told me to get out of the area and to go home to my parents and do something with my life. I carry his words forever in me. He started my change on that day.

Although I have made some decisions in my life that have hurt me emotionally, financially, or physically, I always recall his words to me. He will forever be a part of my life. His daughter and I recently reconnected on Facebook. She is a doctor now and lives in California.

Cecilia: I would advise caregivers and loved ones not to be afraid to try to help. I try to help my daughter, but she doesn't let me get close. I feel like the quiet ones hide so much. They're withdrawn. They're the ones who need help.

Carole: What would have helped you?

Cecilia: If I only had someone to tell me to leave him. I just couldn't leave him. I thought he'd kill my daughter if I left. I was so afraid that I wouldn't be able to feed my daughter. That was my worst fear, not to have any food for her.

Sherry: So if someone had told you about the resources and help available . .?

Allison: A lot of people are afraid to ask.

Cecilia: He knew I didn't have papers. I was here illegally. I could not work. He knew I couldn't get a job or assistance. He tied my hands so I was stuck. That was something else that kept me there. How was I going to work? I stayed because I thought there was no way out.

Allison: Look at all the people you are helping just by telling your story.

Cecilia: There's only so much people can take. If it wasn't for The Second Step helping me get papers, and get custody of the kids, and get my abuser off of my back . . . It was a lot to go through, but I was not alone. Once you have support, you feel safe.

Carole: Of course it was hard. You had never been on your own before. First you were dependent on the family you worked for when you first came to Boston, and then you were dependent on two different abusers.

Cecilia: I think a lot of women go through this, but don't talk about it. There's a fear of what can be taken away from you, especially the kids. He used to threaten to call immigration, and he accused me of kidnapping the kids. When you have to go before the judge, somehow you find the resilience to do what you need to do. Like when I was sleeping in the car . . . I did what I had to do. I found the strength. No mother will allow her child to be taken without a fight. If I hadn't had the support, I think I would have gone crazy. I would have broken. The fact that my advocates knew about law . . . the fact that I had somebody sitting next to me in the courtroom . . . it was so helpful. Especially when just being in the building was scary.

I'm sad that my abusers took so much from me, but I'm still in one piece. If I see anyone having problems, I hope I can help. I hope I can point them to the right place. One day, I will.

Sherry: I don't doubt that you will. The ripple effect will be profound.

Donna-Marie: The immigration piece is so challenging. It will be helpful to people to know there is a way through it.

Cecilia: Even though the courtroom is so scary and when you're there your hands are freezing ice, when the lawyers come to you they are humans. The lawyer wrote up the paperwork with my story. But I don't remember much. I was there but I was not there. I was invisible.

Olive: When I was at the immigration office, I started to feel the guilt worrying about what was going to happen to him. Going through the affidavits and police records was one of the hardest things I had done. I kept thinking that it was my fault, that I shouldn't have been doing this.

Sherry: And his mom was so "good" at making you feel guilty, when what you needed was for someone to support you through this.

Olive: It wasn't until a year or so later that he knew that I'd tried to get him deported. He was never supposed to know about this, but he somehow found out.

PART III

GET HEALED:
Moving From Surviving
To Thriving

Whispers from A Sister

DON'T BE AFRAID TO SAY "NO."

Cut yourself some slack. There will be ups and downs.
COVER YOUR TRACKS.

Keep trusting and believing.

Make choices about who you want to be with.

Focus on self-care. Find whatever works for you, whether baths, medication, make-up, or high heels.

Accept and acknowledge the goodness in yourself.

ACCEPT THE COMPLIMENTS THAT COME YOUR WAY. REALLY HEAR AND ABSORB THEM.

DON'T BE AFRAID TO GO IT ALONE. *Laughter is healing.*

Let in the good stuff. Allow yourself to see what others are trying to help you to see.

ACKNOWLEDGE YOUR INNER STRENGTH AND POWER.

Find your path in the midst of the chaos.

Tell your story over and over. Tell it as many times as you need, and then release it.

Expect the journey to be tough and plan accordingly.

Stay true to yourself.

If you have to confront your abuser in court, expect it to be tough. Bring a friend or some sort of talisman to ground you, to remind you of how strong you are now, and to pull you up out of any triggered responses you may have when you see the asshole.

TELL YOUR STORY.

Peel back the pain and hurt one layer at a time.

Healing begins when you're not by yourself. Find women with similar experiences and share your stories, your laughter, and your pain.

An Imperfect System

*"You just put this behind you and start your new life
and he pops up again, like Satan."*

— Allison

*"It's awful. You're sitting there across from someone you are already
afraid of. You sit there shaking in fear. The only thing that comes out
of your mouth is babble."*

— Donna-Marie

We have come a long way from the days when standard police protocol for domestic violence was to instruct an abuser to take a walk around the block to cool off. Fortunately, the justice system is becoming more attuned to the special needs inherent in domestic violence situations. In Massachusetts, for example, police officers carry a "Domestic Violence Protocol" card to help them assess danger levels and to better equip them to ferret out the truth in the midst of a stressful situation. And many courts, though not all, now have specially trained Victim Witness Advocates.

But while some courts are progressive, others remain rooted in the "old-school" thinking about domestic violence as an internal family problem. There is still marked inconsistency from court to court, and from advocate to advocate. As Carole tells the group, progress is being made, but it is occurring on the backs of women who have already been seriously harmed, even killed.

She recounts the horrifying story of Tracey Thurman—a Connecticut wife and mother who had taken out a restraining order on her husband back in the 1980s. He phoned from the driveway of her house, insisting she come out and speak with him. Tracey made numerous calls to the police over a span of 45 minutes before they finally agreed to come. Tracey was outside when they arrived. The officers, unsure how to proceed in what they could see was clearly a domestic dispute, remained in their car while Tracey was severely beaten before their eyes. Tracey survived, but only barely. She was left paralyzed. The public was justifiably outraged, and from Tracey's case came important changes to the legislation and police protocols. We now have the Thurman Law, instituted in Connecticut in 1986, calling for mandatory arrests in wife-beating cases; and, in separate legislation, *all* police officers are now required to have domestic violence training.

The group checks in . . .

Olive is buoyant, filled with enthusiasm for the playground she has just finished constructing for her business. "I did the measuring and ordering of the materials. I did it on my own. There's new grass. There's an L-shape space with wood chips. There's an area for the kids to garden. I put in a fence so people can hear us but not see us. I put in a little patio and a little brick square and a walkway." There is justifiable pride in her voice as she recounts the steps she's taking to improve and expand her business.

Allison arrives late. She is in the middle of final exams, working 60-hour weeks at her job, doing her best to be a great mom to her three kids, all while keeping her grades up so she can maintain her scholarships. She jokes that sleep is optional these days. She has one year of school remaining.

Becca nods in understanding. Like Allison, she too had once been awarded the One Family Scholarship for Formerly Homeless

Mothers. Ultimately, she had to drop the scholarship—and her classes—because she was unable to meet all of One Family's requirements. There is a lot of pressure for scholarship recipients to attend meetings and comply with a full-time course load, which for Becca, with a young and disabled child at home, had become too much of a time commitment.

Selma also arrives late and is clearly upset. It doesn't take the group long to learn why. Her lawyer called to let her know that her abuser was summoning her back into court. "His agenda is to make me look like a raging lunatic," she says. "I've spent the last two days in total depression. I have a lot of battles coming at me in so many ways, but I'm staying optimistic, because I have to. I have to pull myself up, for my son."

"He's claiming that I kidnapped my son. So I have criminal charges against me and kidnapping charges. He even filed charges that I threatened him! This from the man who used to beat me daily. He's coming full force. I'm fighting back. My biggest fear is that he knows where I am. I look for him constantly. I'm scared to open the window at night because I'm afraid he's going to come in. I am terrified. Part of me wants to run, like I've always done. That's my make-up. The other part of me says, my son is grounded in his school, and it's time to stop running."

Allison: Are you on Section 8?

Selma: I'm going to apply to get some help.

Allison: I'm sorry you have to go through this.

Selma: Well, how long can I run?

Allison: At some point you say, enough is enough. I'm ready to fight. If I don't fight now, then he wins.

Carole: How can we help with safety planning?

Selma: I'm going to look into moving, in the next month or two. Moving so I feel safer. I'm paying $1,000/month in rent and now they're asking for an additional $150 for utilities. I don't know what I'll do. It's hard to live knowing that somebody wants to kill you. So if I die, it's been nice knowing all of you.

Carole: What about a restraining order?

Selma: That makes it worse, actually.

Sherry: Do you have a record of him having abused you? Is that all documented?

Selma: There were times I went to the emergency room and he got away with it, because I didn't say a lot, because I didn't believe in the judicial system. I regret that now. But he is wanted in Rhode Island, so that's a good thing.

Sherry: What about the time he decapitated the cat? Is that documented?

Selma: Yes, my boss called and filed a report so it is documented, thanks to her. Hopefully everything will take its course and make me stronger, and then I'll be able to give back in a way that I should have been given to a long time ago.

Carole: What's his Rhode Island warrant for?

Selma: He threatened the church, and he threatened to kill me. The police have all the tape recordings of it, but they don't seem too concerned because it happened in Rhode Island, not Boston.

I am going to look into getting some kind of rent subsidy so I won't have to worry about the rent so much. I'm having such a hard time getting through the days. We'll see. But I'm happy

I'm here tonight, and that my son's okay. He knows a bit about what's going on, and he knows what precautions to take.

Allison: You just put this behind you and start your new life and he pops up again, like Satan.

Selma: No matter how much we heal, we don't have time to sit back and breathe. The devastation is constant. When will it end?

Carole: You've made all this progress, but now you're getting sucked back into the vortex again.

Selma: My big goal is to go to work, pay my bills, and go to bed by 9:00 every night.

Allison: Have you ever thought about leaving Massachusetts?

Selma: I'm tired of running.

Sherry: You brought yourself to a point of strength. You'll get back there again.

Allison: Alice Walker's book, *The Color Purple,* has helped me so many times. Miss Celie took a while to find her voice. She found it in the end. I watch the movie once a month. It was a bumpy road, with lots of detours. Miss Celie is my hero.

Carole: Selma, I can hear your frustration and despair. Even though this is awful and retriggering, you're *not* back there. You're in a safe place.

Selma: I think when you're robbed of so much, it changes you. I'm hoping I can help others at some point, but my main goal is to raise my son.

I don't really feel I can rely on the police. Some police officers are abusers themselves. Personally, I don't trust them.

Olive: Whenever I go into court, it brings up all the bad memories for me. When the police first come to the house, you tell the truth. It's only later that you come up with a cover story.

Selma: He tried to kill me with his car, yet they arrested us both. You can't blame me for not trusting police officers.

Carole: Many of us have been brought up to think that the police will help. But it's so complicated. Survivors think they'll go into court and get justice. It doesn't necessarily happen that way. Going to court can be a very traumatic experience for survivors. They have to face their abuser, who is often suave, manipulative, and charismatic. Because of the trauma, the survivor may present as overly emotional and irrational, putting her credibility into question with the judge.

Donna-Marie: It's awful. You're sitting there across from someone you are already afraid of. You sit there shaking in fear. The only thing that comes out of your mouth is babble.

Selma: You're broken. You start to feel crazy. You're a total wreck, and this calm, cool, collected person says, "I love her. That's the mother of my children." They are so poised and together, and we look disheveled and in need of meds.

Becca: The night he beat the crap out of me, I finally went to court. I had whiplash and was in a lot of pain. I had to get from Norwood to Dedham on the bus to get a restraining order. It was demeaning, a nightmare. I was 24-years-old at the time. I did get the restraining order, and he got probation. Later he took a knife to some woman's throat, and he did go to jail for that. He is now in and out of jail, and I get notices from the court alerting me so I can keep safe.

Olive: I feel like the police officers in this community don't mess around. They know what to do. They pulled me outside so they could speak to me privately. They wouldn't let me hide. They drove me to the hospital.

Selma: I had a restraining order. He came into my home anyway. He filled my oven with lighter fluid. He left threatening messages on my answering machine. The police came and just told me to clean everything up. They did nothing.

He used to call the police to tell them that our son was in danger. This forced them to come and disrupt my life. They'd laugh when I'd tell them about the restraining order. They'd say, "Maybe this isn't the town for you." Then they'd start harassing *me.*

Cecilia: Even when I did press charges and went to the police, he convinced me to drop the charges.

Sherry: You were so brainwashed. You thought you were the bad one, not him.

Cecilia: He said, "You made me do it." It goes back to my grandmother, who said, "My husband doesn't love me anymore." When we asked her why she felt that way, she responded, "Because he doesn't beat me anymore." It's not uncommon in the Hispanic community for a mother to tell her daughter, "You don't have an abuser, you have a husband."

Carole: This all sounds pretty daunting. What would you recommend to a sister or a friend who was going through this?

Olive: Give them positive messages. Tell them to keep going. If they don't get the right officer or counselor the first time, find another one. Communities are now putting together these "dangerousness teams," so different departments are now talking to each other.

No More Secrets

> The Jenny Geiger Crisis Center, with a grant from The U.S. Department of Justice Office on Violence Against Women, has created a national model for Domestic Violence High Risk Teams. This model is built on three strategies: 1: Assessing lethality (based on the work of Dr. Jacquelyn Campbell); 2: monitoring high risk cases and sharing information by a multi-disciplinary team that includes partners from law enforcement, prosecution, hospitals, and batterer intervention programs; 3: implementing case-specific programs to reduce the danger.

Sherry: Hold firm to the fact that you're not crazy; you're right.

Becca: I felt like it was safe to call the hotlines.

Selma: Yes, but then you always have to remember to dial another number afterwards, so he won't see the hotline on the display as the last number dialed.

The group, collectively: We have to emphasize the importance of safety planning throughout this book.

There's Nothing Broken
That Can't Be Fixed

"We come in feeling like victims.
Now we don't feel like victims any more.
I finally see what my true strength is."

– Olive

There is a full house tonight. Even Amber, who has only attended one other meeting, is here. It feels good to have the conference room full, with every chair occupied and all the women "leaning in" — eager, engaged, and ready to get started. This level of attendance has become increasingly rare, as the women are each so busy with jobs, school, children, and the challenges of everyday life. It can be hard to carve out the time to come to meetings. It can feel like a luxury, an indulgence even, in the midst of everyone's ever-growing "to do" list. But once the women arrive they are happy to have made the effort and in most cases greatly benefit from having done so.

Tonight's meeting commences with a handout. With much fanfare, Carole presents each woman with the professional photograph that had been taken at The Second Step's recent "Day of Beauty." This is an annual event that Sherry organizes, bringing in local massage therapists, manicurists, make-up artists, and hair stylists who volunteer their services. There is an abundance of delicious food, childcare for the kids, and an army of professionals all there for the sole purpose of making the women of The Second Step Nurturing Groups and Narrative Healing Group feel beautiful inside and out. The women's reactions to their portraits vary widely and in a way serve as a metaphor for where each one is in her journey away from abuse.

The group checks in . . .

Olive: When I look at this picture, I feel like myself. I feel untouchable, stronger. The picture looks the way I feel. I see such a difference between my photo this year and the one from last year. I'm a new person. More solid. For ten years, I didn't look in a mirror. When I finally did, I realized I had pretty skin.

I see growth by leaps and bounds. I'm comfortable that I've owned the abuse. It's serious, but I'm still in one piece, so why not keep going? I know there will be other storms, but I'm equipped now to handle them.

I feel like I'm in command of my own destiny. Everything is falling into place. I look back and see where I've come from and realize somebody was looking after me. Something was working on my behalf. Doors kept opening for the last few years. I'm driving the ship now.

The job I'm doing now is what I'm supposed to be doing. I feel a real connection to my work.

Cecilia: Not me. I look at my picture and feel old and tired, like he took the best out of me. I still have a long way to go.

The group asks Cecilia to consider that the best had not been taken from her, that it was still within her. She shakes her head no.

Selma: I don't like my picture. It's not a reflection of where I want it to end. Like a part of me has vanished. Like something was robbed along the way. Personally and spiritually I still have a way to go. Do you ever get it back? So much was robbed.

The group says, collectively: So much was robbed *without permission!*

Olive: You will get there. You will know the abuse is there, but you won't focus on it so much. You move forward.

Becca: I didn't like my picture the first year. But this year my photo is light and airy. When I saw it, my first thought was, "This is my author photo."

Allison: My first thought when I saw my photo was, "I need to eat. I'm too skinny!" I see a work in progress, but I'm happy with where I am. I want to see the glass as half full, but I still see areas to work on. Life is good. I am happy. I have a pretty smile. I'm coming out of my shell. Slowly, but I am. I'm really happy to have this photo. There are no photos of me as a child.

Donna-Marie: Day of Beauty was overwhelming for me. There were so many people wanting to help me. I had never been in a place where people were fighting to get to me — but in a good way. I don't think my picture really looks like me. Selma and I were just goofing for the camera. This picture isn't me; it's too girly-girly.

Selma: When I look at this picture, I see the exhaustion of having to constantly do battle. If it wasn't for my son, I don't think I'd do it anymore.

Carole: This is your opportunity to redefine yourself.

Cecilia: I don't know how to fix it. I feel in the middle of the woods, lost. I go up hills, down hills, and then it's totally dark. The sun comes out again, but I still can't rest, because it starts all over again.

Allison: I let go of the anger. Now I'm wearing make-up and high heels!

Cecilia: I feel like he took the best of me. It was taken and you can't get it back. I was dumb. But I didn't know.

Allison: You weren't stupid. You were in love, and you trusted him.

Cecilia: I don't know how to reclaim my life. I don't drink or smoke, but I eat to numb the pain.

Sherry: Do you let in the messages that we give you, or do you only hear his messages?

Cecilia: Only his.

Selma: Cecelia, I have seen you grow so much in the three years I've known you. You didn't speak at all for the first year of the group. You can't take back the times you were raped and abused, but you have to move on.

Olive: When one door closes another one opens. The Second Step has taught me to keep going. I've learned how to let it go — and how to listen to myself.

Now I have this business that I built. A big part of my life is to give to others. I want to create a fund for battered women. I can't wait to give back in triple what The Second Step has given to me. I want my donations and effort to be anonymous. I want to do magic undercover.

Selma: I don't want to move anymore.

Olive: I gave up my Section 8 housing assistance, and, I have to tell you, it feels good. But you have to know what you're doing. I was still really anxious about setting aside a stash of money somewhere. There is a lot at stake without that support. I work harder than ever now, but I feel like I'm part of something meaningful.

Sherry: There's a part of you that's feeling really proud, and another part feels anxious.

Olive: I got so focused on housework that I found I wasn't enjoying the kids. So I hired somebody to spend one hour each week pulling the house together for me. But I felt guilty that I wasn't doing my share of the work so I'd let her go early but still pay her for the full time. But, I'm better with this now. It's hard to spend that money, but it gives me peace of mind. She comes twice a week now. I'm happier now. It's working.

But I won't let the kids call her the "help." I tell them that she works with me, that she's my assistant. I don't tell people that I have a housekeeper. When I did tell someone, she said, "You're like a white woman now." That felt nasty. I'm just a caregiver.

Carole: You're an entrepreneur!

Olive: I don't have the status of the families that I used to nanny for.

Carole and Sherry, together: That's not true! Why are you any different?

Sherry: I'd like to hear you say that you're an entrepreneur and that you have your own business. Own your success.

Olive: It's nice to be able to pay my bills. But I'm still a teacher and a seeker. I don't want status. I just want to be me. I don't want anyone to know anything.

Selma: You sound like you have it so well balanced. There are so many people who have money and they just want to flaunt it.

Allison: You're better than me. If I come into some money I'm buying Christian Louboutin shoes and going on a Coach purse shopping spree!

Olive: If I ever got a Coach purse it would sit in my closet. My splurging is on friends and having good times. I don't need no Mercedes and all that stuff. Well, maybe a Mercedes.

Carole: That's what's so special about you. You're authentic.

Olive: I can now look in the mirror and know there's nothing broken that can't be fixed.

Carole: And I'm noticing determination in your voice. Your voice is louder.

Olive: People can actually hear me when I speak on the phone now.

Selma: I have been studying for my real estate license. I need a way to earn a lot of money fast. I'll specialize in rentals and sales in Newton and Belmont and Watertown. I finish the class Friday and will take the test on Wednesday.

Imagine five years from now where we'll be. I'll be making a difference, that's for sure.

Carole: You'll all be published authors, for one. We'll be in the audience, and you'll be up there talking on the stage.

Selma: That would be the ultimate I could do to my ex-husband. After all these years of running in fear, to be able to show him, here I am now.

Olive: Dr. Phil would be good.

Selma: We rarely do things for us. And that's so important. I haven't been to the hairdresser for 10 years.

Allison: I do things for myself. Once a month I have microdermabrasion and get my toenails done. I get my hair done twice a month. Even though it costs money, I feel good about myself. My professor—Miss Liz—taught me that. If I don't take care of myself, how can I take care of anyone else? Sometimes I go to the movies without the children. I have to do these things. I get depressed when I'm stretched too thin. Miss Liz would instruct me to do something for myself, and then I'd have to go back and report to her what I'd done.

> Self-care is an essential part of the healing process, and helps to build self-love, self-worth, unconditional acceptance, and confidence.
>
> Social worker and trauma expert Lorraine Laffata recommends "Five Practices to a Sustainable Life:"
>
> Renewing Practices—giving back to yourself to renew and refresh your physical, emotional and mental well-being (healthy eating, getting enough sleep, prayer)
>
> Releasing Practices—getting "stuff out" (writing, singing, praying, dancing)
>
> Sweating Practices—getting toxins out of your body (exercise, spicy foods, yoga, steam shower and sauna)
>
> Ecstasy Practices—doing things simply to bring pure JOY to your life (long drives, walks, sex, fun with kids, laughing)
>
> Peace Practices—bringing stillness and peace (meditation, breath, sleep, yoga)

Cecilia: I think I have a cleaning disorder. I'm fighting the stains and at the same time I'm fighting myself. I don't know how to stop it.

Carole: That's a trauma thing.

Cecilia: It's so bad that when anyone else cleans, I have to go check they did it right.

Carole: That's a form of anxiety. It's a compulsion. One of the few things you can control is the way you want your house to be. Everything was so unpredictable before or in such disarray.

Allison: You get it in your head that if you remove this item you'll feel better.

Carole: That's what you're trying to do with your life. Trying to keep it in order and make it all clean and tidy.

Selma: It's one of the few things we can control. We self-medicate.

Olive: One time I was so fed up with my ugly dishes that I threw them all away. Then I had to go back into the trash and dig them out again because we had no dishes to use!

Selma: Do you think we go through phases? Like we're on a rollercoaster? When do we get off? At some point it has to stop affecting us.

Sherry: My guess is that you'll go longer and longer between those difficult phases.

Selma: I know people who are thirty years down the road from abuse and they still jump.

Carole: I'm wondering if trauma therapy would help to give you strategies for calming down.

Olive: Breathing exercises help. I do Xi Gong. It's relaxing. It's a way to channel the stress and push out all the negativity.

Allison: It also helps to reach out to your friends. I still depend on the women I lived with at The Second Step. We are there for each other and check in every six months or so.

Amber: I feel like I still don't know how to take care of myself, but I'm great at taking care of everyone else. I can't even tell you what my favorite food is.

Selma: I see a strong woman, someone who always looks well put together.

Amber: The façade never changes. I make sure of that. I have always been a diva, a high-heeled, dress-up fool. I do believe there is a purpose to all of this in my life: meeting you great women, learning to deal with the mental health resources for my kids. Navigating the domestic violence system has helped me with that. I do think some type of advocacy work is in my future.

Navigating New Relationships

"I no longer want to rescue another man again.
I have no more life preservers to offer.
They'll have to think about that before they get on the boat."
— **Becca**

The group is regrouping, so to speak—using Amber's renewed presence as an opportunity to refocus and reaffirm what brought everyone together in the first place. The first order of business tonight is to restate the group's goals and the ground rules for achieving them.

Surprisingly, though, what started out as a quick exercise to kick off the meeting winds up being the meeting in its own right and prompts some interesting discussion about the new relationships that have cropped up in a few of the women's lives. It turns out that some of the key rules for the group—respect each other, be honest, help, encourage, and validate each other—would actually serve as pretty good ground rules for any relationship.

The group checks in . . .

Olive: I'm learning some new things about the man in my life. His life is an open book. I am still trying to figure out his personality, his attention span, and whether he has a short fuse or not. I wouldn't say he's my boyfriend at this point.

Selma: Do you think you can ever really truly know those red flags?

Carole: Yes. Once you've been through what you all have been through, and you know those dynamics, then yes. If you're honest with yourself and you're looking for those red flags, then you'll see them.

Olive: You can't miss them.

Allison: This man at school wants to date me, and he tries to bully me, and he's obnoxious. I know I wouldn't have a voice with him.

Selma: I wrack my brain thinking about what I'd seen, the signs I missed.

Olive: I don't think there's a person in the world that could manipulate me now. You just have to pay attention. Ask yourself the questions.

Selma: But when you're asking the questions, they give you the answers you want to hear! They're master manipulators.

Carole: A key feature to look for is real empathy. Abusive personalities are narcissistic as hell. They do things to make themselves look good, not to do something special for you.

Selma: So, you mean if they don't do anything nice for you …?

Carole: If they don't do anything empathic. If they don't truly, selflessly care for you, really focus on you — not all the time, but when appropriate.

Selma: When I would be out with my abuser, if anyone bothered me he would be so protective. It was like he didn't want anyone else to hurt me, because *he* wanted to be the one to kill me.

Carole: Jealousy is a big flag, too. It's about not messing with my property.

Selma: I'd fall down, and he'd come running and help me. But he'd beat me at home, so I don't know why he felt compelled to help me in public.

Allison: It's giving that perception to people out there that he's a good guy. We give a picture of a perfect family, but once we're home he's the monster I should be afraid of.

Selma: I didn't see any signs, and I think about that a lot.

Carole: Another huge warning sign is rushing the relationship — rushing to have sex, rushing to move in together. All of a sudden, they own you. You're inseparable. You have no personal space. And at first, that can be intoxicating — "Oh my God, he must really like me" — when in fact that should be a huge red flag. Anyone who is not respectful of your boundaries in that way, who is forcing himself upon you, is someone to watch out for.

Selma: I'm just going to vet any future men through you.

Carole: They get to know you fast. They figure out your vulnerabilities.

Selma: But how do you differentiate that?

Sherry: It's about timing, about letting it unfold. Your gut will tell you if you're feeling manipulated.

Selma: I rush into things. That's just my personality. I'm going to think about that. I have someone in my life now whom I love, but he's boring. I miss the drama. I find myself trying to start fights with him, to rev him up.

Sherry: Give yourself permission to experiment with different types of relationships.

Donna-Marie: I believe in that expression, that people come into our lives for "a reason, a season, or a lifetime."

Allison: In my past relationships, I've always been a savior. If I met a guy now who had both a job *and* a car, it would seem strange. That's just not normal to me. Everyone I've dated has been an unemployed felon. They always needed my car. That's why I'm going through this period of time when I'm not dating. Because I need to separate out the old Allison and determine what my value is. I didn't see myself as someone who was worthy of dating someone who had a job. I have to reteach myself that I do have value, that I am worthy, that I am this beautiful person who deserves happiness and someone to love me. I'm open to the dating thing, but I want to be careful about who I bring home to my kids. One man was sweet to me, but then was rude to my kids.

Olive: One man I dated told me he was too busy and would make time for me later. I said fine, that I was busy, too. Then when he wasn't busy, he got very persistent about wanting my time. Everything had to be on his agenda.

Allison: I don't have time to date right now. Everything is so busy with my job. I hadn't realized I had put in more than 100 hours over the last two weeks. I have to pull back. School is more important to me, and all that time working is time I'm not spending with my kids.

My son is struggling in school, and I'm working too many hours to be able to help him. Work can't be my focus right now. The money is great, but it will come later, after I have my education. I have to give my kids some time.

I'm starting to be more aware of bad habits I'm picking up. I'm drinking a lot of coffee, which is making me wired. I have to take Tylenol PM at night in order to unwind. And my kids have started to ask if I have a problem with wine. It used to be that I wouldn't drink around my kids. But now I'm more open about it. The wine bottles are collecting on the counter. Even my four-year-old will come and hand me my wine. That is not good.

At times I feel like I'm Superwoman and can take on the world, but in reality I'm doing too much and taking on too many responsibilities. I have to be better about saying "no."

Sherry: Just listen to that voice in you. That's a smart voice.

Allison: I'm trying to pay more attention to the signs. I'm a work in progress. I'm not Superwoman. I need to stop pretending that I can handle everything. And I want to start showing my children more emotion. When I was growing up, crying was a sign of weakness. I need to cry more in front of my children, or just show them emotion. I see that my four-year-old is having a hard time showing emotion, and it's really hard for him to say he's sorry. He's getting that from me. I want my children to be comfortable showing their weak side. I still can't cry in front of my siblings.

Selma: When did you begin to feel it was okay to show emotion in front of your kids?

Allison: I think I just got tired of hiding it. I hid my emotions for so long. I have past addictions that I've dealt with. I snorted cocaine, and I would drink vodka out of the bottle. I'd be in the movie theater with one of those purse-sized bottles.

I'm glad my kids are comfortable telling me they think I'm drinking a lot of wine.

I actually love being a single parent. I make it so much fun for my kids, they don't even think about not having a dad. I would rather be alone and happy than have my kids tell me they weren't happy with a man I brought home.

Selma: It's still hard for me to understand, given how this man crumbled my world, how I still felt a need to run to him. If I had not had The Second Step tools — the supportive meetings, knowing Carole is just a phone call away, knowing it's not OK to be raped, beaten, cut by one's partner — then I probably would have gone back to him.

But he hasn't changed at all. He would offer to buy my son new sneakers, but only if I would agree to go to dinner with him.

He did apologize. Finally. After fifteen years. And only because his mother pushed him to do it.

Becca: I am learning the tools to negotiate a successful relationship, but I still have a way to go. I mean, where do I find these people? I don't exactly feel like a walking target, and yet . . . I cycle between high self-esteem and low self-esteem.

For years, I thought he would change, or that I could rescue him. I no longer have that feeling. It's gone. I no longer want to rescue another man again. I have no more life preservers to offer. They'll have to think about that before they get on the boat. I'm keeping the life preservers for me and for Kayla.

All I can say is that I want to know what a real relationship is. I don't think I've ever been in one. Right now I'm worried about turning into a crazy cat lady, but for now I'm limiting my cats to two!

Amber: My husband was always more interested in being a husband than a father. He has recently started to be threatening again, because I've started dating another man. My son told him, and he popped a gasket. When I was able to say to him, "Get the fuck out of my house," I knew I had my strength back.

This journey has humbled me so badly. I have had to kiss a lot of ass these last few years.

Like Selma said, there's a part of you that still wants him in your life, because you want your children to have a father. But my kids are now 20 and 21. That time is past. I actually think he hated the kids. He was jealous of them.

Donna-Marie: I kind of feel like an addict. There are days when I just feel I need something, or someone. No matter how much I say I deserve better, I'm like a magnet. And the next relationship is exactly what I had before. You don't realize it at first. But then there are those early warning signs and before you know what's happened, you're right back in an abusive relationship.

Olive: My situation is so similar. Why do we still even let them in the door? After all they did to us?

Donna-Marie: I took my mom to lunch at Olive Garden so I could tell her about the publication of my book, *How Can I Forgive if I Can't Forget?* I don't know how she didn't know about it. She was so excited that one of her kids wanted to take her out. But once we sat down, I realized I wouldn't be able to say what I needed to say to her. I simply couldn't find the courage. I was afraid I'd burst into tears right there in the restaurant. It didn't help that our waiter knew me. He was a kid I had once coached in basketball.

It wasn't until we were driving home that I mustered the strength to tell her not only about the publication of the book, but also about its contents. I pulled into a random driveway and started to talk. I told her about the incest, the rapes, the police officer. There was a lot she says she didn't know, though she remembered the police officer.

No one in the group knows this part of Donna-Marie's story. When Carole asks her to elaborate, she pauses, as if unsure, and then resumes speaking.

Donna-Marie: I ran away to the police station when I was in middle school. I had gotten kicked out of camp and knew I was going to get in trouble big time with my adopted family. I told the officer what happened and what was going to happen. He took me to his house. He made me believe that he was contacting my birth parents, so I sat around waiting. I fell asleep, and when I woke up my pants were down around my ankles. He drove me home and told me not to tell anyone. "Who are they going to believe," he said, "a lying little bitch or a police officer?"

I remember all the details of his house, but not a thing about how I got there, or the outside of the house, or the drive home. Nothing.

The saddest part is that when I began to tell this story as an adult, nobody believed me, not even my family.

I sat in that car with my mom and talked and shared all the pain and memories from my childhood. She could only respond by saying, over and over, "All this happened in *my* house?"

I explained to her that that was why I'd had to leave. There was no way I could heal in that house. I tried to explain the impact of her abuse. All she did was beat me. As a result, I went into the world convinced I was unlovable.

Allison: At least you got to tell your mom while she was still alive. I wish I'd had that chance.

Amber: I had to let my issues with my mom go. She has Alzheimer's now, so what does it matter? In spite of my feelings towards her, and towards my brother, who was also abusive, I still have custody of his child. Why should this kid be denied a chance just because his dad is a monster?

Donna-Marie: I'm not sure if I got through to my mother or not. She did sit and listen. I reminded her of how brutal her beatings were. They went on and on, because I didn't cry enough. I'd holler and scream, but she wouldn't stop until she saw tears. If she didn't beat me, she'd put me in a cold bleach bath. I was just relieved to be sitting in water.

Whenever she beat me or my siblings, we had to pick our own switches.

Allison: Yep, us too . . . Water hoses, brooms, shoes . . .

Donna-Marie: I got beat with a pot once—a cast iron one. I remember just protecting my head. That was when I broke my wrist. I never went to the doctor for that.

Carole: The South was the last place in the country to change the rule that the switch a man uses in a beating cannot be wider than the circumference of his thumb—that's where the expression "rule of thumb" comes from. It was an English King's rule, which was meant to be compassionate towards women. All over the South it was a common practice, applied to both animals and wives.

According to the Minnesota Center Against Violence and Abuse's, "Herstory of Domestic Violence," during the reign of Romulus in Rome, wife beating was accepted and condoned under The Laws of Chastisement. These laws gave the husband absolute rights to physically discipline his wife with a switch, provided the switch was not wider than the circumference of his thumb. The tradition of these laws was perpetuated in English Common Law and throughout most of Europe. The "finger-switch" rule was renounced in 1874, when the Supreme Court of North Carolina ruled that "the husband has no right to chastise his wife under any circumstances."

Donna-Marie: I somehow managed to break the cycle of violence with my daughter. I didn't hit her once during her childhood. I think if I had, I would not have been able to stop.

Carole: Have your feelings about being a magnet for abusive relationships changed?

Donna-Marie: Like Selma, I'm not willing to put up with people's crap. Even now, in my current relationship, it's all on my terms. I actually feel sorry for my girlfriend. If I don't want to see her on the weekend, she doesn't get to see me. I don't know if that's bad or good, but it's what I need right now. But it's different from my previous relationship, because she respects my space. When I say "I need time to breathe," she gives it to me.

Sherry: It also sounds like you're testing a bit, to see what happens when you push the boundaries.

Olive: That's why I'm not sure I want a relationship now. It would be unfair for anyone coming into my life right now. With my female friends, I can be truthful and if I'm upset can gently tell them how I feel. That's what we've created here.

Where We Are Now

*"I feel empowered by this process. He told the story,
and now I'm writing a new story."*

— Selma

*"I would never have believed that I would come to trust you guys.
This is the greatest number of friends I've ever had."*

— Donna-Marie

*"It's not an Olympics of pain. It's not about whose pain is worse.
It's about what you've endured."*

— Carole

It is late fall. Tonight the wind is brisk and the air has a decided bite. One by one the women come in from the chill to the warmth and camaraderie of the Narrative Healing Group.

Sherry has brought Italian Wedding soup and Kale and Sweet Potato soup for our dinner, made by a local restaurateur who is also a domestic violence survivor. There is something symbolic and poetic and downright wonderful about her delicious food nourishing other survivors.

Cecilia, Selma, Olive, Becca, Allison, and Donna-Marie eat and chatter about their latest adventure together. There is no denying that the women of this group have transcended their roles of fellow survivors coming together for weekly sessions and have become, in fact, friends.

There is compelling research demonstrating that a sense of community is one of the most critical paths to healing and moving on with one's life. For Carole and Sherry to see these women supporting each other as they do, outside of the group, is a wondrous development. It doesn't surprise them; this is the intent of the Narrative Healing Group, after all. But it delights them nonetheless to see it happening right before their eyes.

At this point, the group has been working on this book for more than two years. Tonight is the final check in before the book project formally ends and the editing and revision process begins.

The group checks in . . .

A discussion prompt is posed one final time: "How is everyone doing?"

The women respond to the prompt with a long silence and a few nervous laughs, an uncharacteristic response for these women who are now so comfortable together. "How is everyone doing?" is not, on its face, a difficult question. But the silence begins to border on uncomfortable. It may be that the women realize they are writing the final pages of the book, and they may feel self-conscious about not having neat, happy endings. Rather, each of their stories is still being written. Finally, Olive begins to speak: "I have mixed feelings," she says slowly, her voice trailing off.

Selma: Not me. I'm much stronger. I miss the dreams of the happily ever after, but I'm content where I am. I am very in tune with what I will and will not accept. I've found self-love. I am still dealing with many, many court issues, to the point that even my freedom is at stake — and this from someone who won't even jay walk! I have come to realize that I still have a way to go. There is much healing that still needs to occur. My abuse was severe, and I am lucky to be alive. I am free for once in a very long time, and I would not change that for the world. I now go to bed knowing I will not be punched or raped as I sleep. I know I have the strength to deal with what lies ahead.

Psychologist Dr. Kristin Neff states that an essential part of healing from trauma is learning self-compassion. They idenify three components to self compassion: 1: self-kindness, which means that when things go wrong we need to treat ourselves with warmth and caring 2: a sense of common humanity, recognizing that we are not alone 3: mindfulness, being open to painful experiences "with non-reactive, balanced awareness."

Allison: I am doing well at this point. I am having the usual ups and downs, but it is more up than down. I have completed my undergraduate degree in social work and I've just been accepted into a three-year Masters of Social Work program.

Olive: I have more clarity. But I have to keep reassuring myself that I'm okay, that I'm fine, that I'm doing what I should be doing. I'm into myself. I'm selfish. I'm taking time for me. I don't want anyone invading my space. I don't want the distraction.

Carole: That sounds like self-esteem to me. You're putting yourself first, and asking for what you need.

Becca: I have ten courses left in my program. I had been signed up for "Research Methods and Math for Liberal Arts Majors" last semester, but then I got hit with Kayla's diagnosis. She has a rare condition known as Peroventricular Nodular Heterotopia (PVNH). It manifests as seizures, learning disabilities, and connective tissue disorders … all of which Kayla has.

It is a relief to have a diagnosis. But I had to put my education on hold. For now, I have to be home caring for Kayla. I'm also dealing with my Post-Traumatic Stress Disorder. It's often overlooked in the domestic violence community, but I can tell you that it's something I cope with daily.

My hope is that once Kayla is stable I can continue with my studies. I feel called to do some type of advocacy work, to help families dealing with trauma and families with disabled children.

Despite the blow of Kayla's diagnosis, which I have to admit really felt like a setback, I am grateful for all that I have in my life. As much as possible, I take time to enjoy my hobbies. I love photography and organic cooking, and I continue to enjoy my work as a member of the board of directors of The Second Step. I was just elected secretary of the board—a position that is part of the executive team. I am honored and excited about this new chapter in my life.

Donna-Marie: I thought doing this work by myself would be better than doing it with a group. I remember thinking I didn't need to be here.

Allison: I'm glad you joined this group. I felt like I was the odd person out because my domestic violence situation only lasted three months. So when you joined it made it easier for me because, like me, you had other abuse. Now I know that getting your behind kicked for three months or ten years is the same. In a way I'm proud of my three months but I knew I needed to get away. I was done with ALL the abuse.

Carole: You had such incredible trauma growing up. That abuse was only the last abusive relationship you experienced. It's not an Olympics of pain. It's not about whose pain is worse. It's about what you've endured. You experienced something that was overwhelming, and you overcame it.

Donna-Marie: That's what's special about our book. We each represent a different experience. Different readers will identify with different parts of our stories. Our stories may touch people.

Carole: Has the process of writing this book helped?

Donna-Marie: It's helped me. I finally have female friends. I thought you'd all be a bunch of cackling hens and all gossipy. But that's not what this is about at all. It's about sharing our lives and common experiences. It's helped me build trust.

This is the only group where I invest my time. I've never before been in a circle of women, never in my life. I would never have believed that I would come to trust you guys. This is the greatest number of friends I've ever had.

As a kid, I never had the dream of a white knight fairy tale. But now, I am starting to think about the fairy tale—like maybe I could have it after all.

Sherry: What changed?

Donna-Marie: When I first came to the group, I could only listen. My trust evolved slowly. Doing the art project together was one of the best things we did. It was great to be at each other's houses.

Also, speaking at Celebrating Success made a big difference to me. If I hadn't stepped forward and done that, I think I would have stayed in the background.

Olive: For me, too. When I was reading my story at Celebrating Success, I saw a man start to cry. A man! Then that made me cry, to see that a stranger could care so much.

Selma: It helped me build a family I didn't have.

Donna-Marie: I like what Selma said, about being comfortable being by yourself or with your kids.

Cecilia: I am strong. I feel like I am the foundation of the house, holding it up. And I do feel like I have matured in my relationships . . .

There is a long pause, and it is clear that Cecilia is struggling with whether or not to continue speaking. The group waits quietly. With the gentlest of prodding from Carole and Sherry, Cecilia starts to speak, choking out the words as she tries to keep tears at bay.

My mother recently told me that I am the child of rape. My father raped her and made her stay with me. I can't speak to her anymore. I don't even know how to approach her.

I see now how things in my life have come full circle. I am a child of rape, then I had a husband who raped me. It's a complete circle. We're just chasing our tails.

Sherry: How do you feel about your father, knowing this?

Cecilia: I have always loved my father, until now. I can't say that I'm sorry. What am I sorry for? But at the same time, I feel unwanted. But, I feel strong, too. I want to be strong.

Carole: There are similarities between your mother's experiences with your dad and your own experiences with your abusers.

Cecilia: I never thought that an American man would be like that. I thought it only happened in Mexico, not here.

I asked my mom, "Why do you continue to stay with him?" And she said, "Where am I going to go?"

That was my story, too. But, while it took me a long time, eventually I did leave. But in the process I damaged my child, that is for sure.

Carole: You didn't damage your child; your abuser did.

Cecilia: No, it was me, because I didn't leave soon enough, so my daughter saw everything.

I wish she could see what she's doing with her life, that she, too, is chasing her tail. I can walk away and avoid an argument with her. She can argue with herself. But it took me years of coming to these meetings to get to this point.

Donna-Marie: My mother was raped by my father as well. It is hard to hear that truth.

Olive: Do you think children should know?

Becca: I would never tell Kayla. What would be the point? We're saying a lot by stopping the cycle.

Cecilia: I agree. You can't do anything about it. You can't undo what's been done.

Becca: When it was happening to me, I was too stressed to do anything about it. You screamed and you got it worse. *Now* I could scream "No."

Donna-Marie: We are made to move forward, to suck it up and keep going. But it's up to us to break the cycle.

Should you tell a child he or she is the child of rape? No way. You just love that child, in spite of you, and in spite of him.

Sherry: So you all are really breaking the cycle. You all have.

Cecilia: I can't tell my mother why I'm not talking to her. It's not my place to hurt her. I'm afraid she'll never let me back in the house.

Becca: I understand that. It hurts to be rejected by your family. I think if I went back and told them all they'd done to me I would just be opening myself up to more rejection.

Selma: But how do you release that anger? You and Cecilia need to find a way to heal that pain, because you didn't do anything wrong.

Becca: I do it by turning my life around, by loving Kayla and by being kind to myself.

Cecilia: I think I'm not from there anymore. I guess now I'm just from here, from this group.

Becca: Our learning has been from each other. It's cumulative. The process has gotten us where we are.

Cecilia: If we stick together, we have more support than we think. As we get together we become stronger. Sometimes even just to touch somebody, even just a hug, it means a lot. For me, this whole process has helped me put my experiences into some kind of order. A lot of stuff is deleted from my memory. It's coming back, but in pieces. It's hard to bring it back together.

Carole: What you're describing is trauma. Common experiences of trauma include numbing and no memories or unclear memories. It all merges in your mind like a monster with two heads. You're starting to dislodge those memories, and it's bringing all this stuff up.

Olive: For me, too, I had to figure out what's real and what's not real. The timing of all of it is going to be off, until it connects.

> Dr. J. Douglas Bremner, at Yale University School of Medicine, writes that trauma has a lasting impact on the hippocampus—the part of the brain relating to memory and emotion. As a result, memory loss, gaps in memory, and time distortion are common characteristics of PTSD.

Cecilia: There's some stuff I don't want to remember. So I skip those things. I try not to think about it. I don't want people to feel sorry for me, but I don't want you to think I'm lying. It's hard to be strong and pretend that there's no pain, when actually you're dying inside. You have to pretend with the kids and with everybody that you're strong, when really inside you're so weak.

He took so much. He took all my childhood. He took everything.

Donna-Marie: Is our being here helpful or not?

Cecilia: It does help, but there's pain. No one can take it away. I think it will always be there. I start to think about it, and I go back to the same place and have that same pain.

Carole: Does the pain ever shift? Do you see it differently?

Cecilia: Yes. I know I'm never going to let it happen again. I'm not shy anymore. At least not as shy! He took the best of my life.

Allison: I don't think so. I think the best is coming. You are fabulous, girl! You gotta see what I see. You gotta step outside of your body!

Donna-Marie: How would you like us to help you tonight? We're not done.

Cecilia: Try to understand that I may have mixed up the characters or the timing or the details. Maybe because in my culture you are only supposed to have one man. If you have more, you are a . . .

Allison: A ho!

Cecilia: That's part of my shame. Truly I believe that both men took the best of my years.

Sherry: How are you feeling about all of this? How are you doing?

Cecilia: This is like a toothache or cavity. You have to go in and extract it, but it hurts. I think I'm just afraid of the pain.

The support helps. We are not alone. We have each other. This process was hard, but it's like you were all holding my hand through it.

With that, the meeting draws to a close. There has been much pain, love and laughter shared in this room over the last few years. As hard as it is to say goodbye to this part of the process, the ending of the book project does not mean the ending of the Narrative Healing Group. In fact, it offers a new beginning. The publication of *No More Secrets* will set the women off on a new journey together, reaching out and speaking out to promote the book, and helping other survivors and their families.

Reflections One Year Later . . .

In the year it has taken to complete the editing process, the women have continued to struggle, to grow, and to change. They now look back at their shared experience with a deeper understanding of the power of healing through connection and sisterhood.

Once again, the women talk about what they've accomplished since they wrote what they thought would be the final chapter of the book, one year ago.

Sherry again tacks an oversized sheet of paper onto the wall and scrawls a question at the top: "How have I grown over the last year?"

There is no hesitation this time. The words come quickly and it is all Sherry can do to keep up.

- I'm in graduate school to get my Licensed Mental Health Counselor degree and have started working as a child clinician. Now that I've healed, I want the outside to reflect the inside. I've lost 68 pounds and feel great.

  — Donna-Marie

- I grew my business and established myself in the community. I'm well known with an excellent reputation. I stood up and told my story to 500 people and received a standing ovation.

  — Olive

- I have melted off 60 pounds of sadness, and have completely taken my life back from the hands of my abusers. I am homeschooling my daughter and am choosing every day to live in the here and now.

  — Becca

- I went back to school and I got licensed as a Certified Nurse's Assistant (CNA). I'm working with private patients in a 4-star, world-class nursing home! I'm living my dream, working with the elderly. My daughter is getting straight A's, and my son worked for the mayor's office this summer.

  — Cecilia

- I reunited with my family and moved back in with my daughter and grandchildren. I hope to launch a sister agency to a non-profit I worked for many years ago. I got my driver's license—I have embraced my fear of driving! I stopped running. My abuser found me, and I didn't run this time. I'm not living in fear anymore. I'm breathing again.

  — Selma

- I am in my second year of graduate school. I continue to volunteer with community programs in Boston.

  — Allison

- I am engaged to be married and I am relocating to Cape Cod—my Florida with snow! I have dreams of opening a Bed and Breakfast someday.

  — Amber

Once everyone has had a chance to speak, Sherry tears off another sheet of paper from the flip chart, tacks it to the wall, and writes a final question: "What have we learned from our journey together?"

Each woman shouts out her answers:

- We all had personal growth. When you carry something so shameful and then you find out that others went through the same thing—that their pain was my pain, then I was finally able to talk about it.

- I feel more secure about telling my story—I feel safer connecting with other people. Prior to this, I was feeling isolated. This drew me out of that place. Once we went through narrative healing, I was more confident and free.

- When I started this book I was in a really bad relationship. I had to get home on time, or my partner would get angry. And now I am out of it.

- This helped me develop empathy for myself. I had empathy for everyone else. It helped me look in the mirror and have compassion.

- I was with everyone in their pain. I felt all of your pain. I got closer in my heart to all of you. We didn't realize how close we are. Within these four walls, we listened to each other's pain.

- We look back now and realize how much we grew. I don't allow anyone to hurt me anymore.

- It built my confidence to be in this group. The group made it possible for me to talk to people. We are all changed. We are more mature.

- This experience helped me to go to school.

- So often people run from pain, but we sat with it and each other. We're stronger for standing with each other. Living everyone else's pain was so hard.

- My image was so distorted for so many years. For so long, I was masking and hiding. Now I can look in the mirror and see me. Now there are other people in the mirror with me.

- We used to look at other people's families. We were on the outside with our children. We envied everyone. We didn't realize how strong we were, until we came here. We kept a roof over our heads. We raised our kids. We kept food on the table, even when we were dying inside. Now we realize we are OK just as we are. Now I'm ok being alone—I don't need a partner. All family make-ups are OK.

- Above everything, I think the thing I feel most accomplished about is that I broke the cycle for my son!

- And my daughter!

- We now have enough strength, peace of mind and awareness to educate our children.

- We so hope some women will be helped by this. We hope survivors will read our book and that we can help them heal.

- Imagine somebody reading this book—where we were then. If only they can imagine—if they could see that they could be their own person, that you can tell your truth.

The noise level grows louder and louder as the women talk over and with each other, everyone laughing and shouting to get her voice heard. Each builds on what the others are saying, encouraging and cheering one another on as they describe the ways in which they've grown. It is magical, listening to the women in the room speak in strong, clear voices resonant with power and pride. There may be more challenges ahead, but tonight is a celebration of all they've accomplished.

The Bond Of Sisterhood
— by Donna-Marie

As I sit at the table, across from the reflection of me;
In my eyes, I see the devastation love has taken
But I also see the hope for resurrection for I am not alone.

As I sit at the table across from the reflection of me;
My heart hurts; my pain is great,
and the tears fall onto my face
I slowly begin to realize that my life was not a disgrace.

As I sit at the table across from the reflection of me;
Many different shades, many different sizes but in our faces
We see,
The same hurt, the same pain and destruction from another
We see that we are no different from our own reflections.

As we sit across the table from the reflection of ourselves;
We begin to bond over a common thread
We begin to heal for a common goal
We begin to see our worth on this earth.

We come here week after week, with struggles, fears.
Hurt and pain. But we also
Know that we are one and the same
Our lives may have led different paths
but our circumstance led us to sit at
This table and engage in deep discussion
Of our past, our hopes, our dreams and our futures

But,
Now as I sit at the table across from the reflection of myself
The sadness in my eyes slowly begins to dissipate
As we begin to heal
Our hearts no longer on our sleeves as a badge of humiliation
But the light within begins to glow
As we begin to build ourselves back up
As we begin to see that our worth is valued
Our love is more valuable than gold
And our bodies and minds are no longer objects for abuse.

As we sit at the table across from the reflection of ourselves
We see beauty, we see hope, we see our common bond
Our common goal
Of happiness from where we are right now
Thankfulness for where we have been in the past
The vision to see that our lives
Are full of possibilities
But most importantly we are free, we are safe
And we have begun to heal at the table sitting across from the
Reflection of ourselves.
This reflection shows the true spirit within each one of us
This refection shows we are determined to succeed
This reflection was the thread that led us to
The bond of sisterhood.

E N D

Appendix

Safety Planning and Other Resources

Help is out there. The following pages list resources available to help survivors recovering from domestic violence — at whatever stage they happen to be in their journey.

Emergency hotlines and informative websites:

- SAFELink Massachusetts Hotline: 877-785-2020

- National Domestic Violence Hotline: 800-799-7233, TTY 800-787-3224

- Boston Area Rape Crisis Center: 800-841-8371

- The Second Step: 617-965-3999 and
  www.thesecondstep.org

- Fenway Health: 617-267-0900 and
  www.fenwayhealth.org

- The Northwest Network: 206-568-7777 and
  www.nwnetwork.org

- The Network La Red Hotline: 617-742-4911,
  TTY 617-227-4911

- Love is Respect (teen domestic violence resources): 866-331-9474 TTY: 866-331-8453, Text: loveis to 22522; www.Loveisrespect.org

- Emerge DV: Batterers Intervention 617-547-9879 and www.emergedv.com

- Abused Deaf Women's Advocacy Service: 855-812-1001 and www.adwas.org

- National Network to End Domestic Violence Resources and listings of coalitions by state: www.nnedv.org

- State-by-state directory of counseling, shelters, legal resources, and domestic violence organizations: www.womenslaw.org

- Rape, Abuse and Incest National Network (RAINN): Hotline 800-656-HOPE (4673) and www.rainn.org

- Jane Doe Inc. Massachusetts Coalition Against Sexual Assault and Domestic Violence: www.janedoe.org

- Sudbury Wayland Lincoln Domestic Violence Roundtable: www.domesticviolenceroundtable.org

Assessing danger and safety planning:

For risk factors for dangerousness and lethality, see Dr. Jacquelyn Campbell's "Danger Assessment Tool:" www.safvic. org/resources/documents/DangerAssessment.pdf

For help with safety planning, go to The National Domestic Violence Hotline: www.thehotline.org/help/path-to-safety

For an Interactive Guide to Safety Planning, go to loveisrespect. org: www.loveisrespect.org/for-yourself/safety-planning

Create a Domestic Violence Safety Plan. (2016). www. safehorizon.org/page/create-a-safety-plan-11.html

Ending the Abusive Relationship. (2008). www.womenslaw.org/ laws_state_type.php?id=13427&state_code=PG#content-13429

Massachusetts Office for Victim Assistance. (2016). www.mass.gov/mova/

National Network to End Domestic Violence. (2009). [Brochure]. nnedv.org/downloads/SafetyNet/OVW/NNEDV_HighTechStalking_Tipsheet_2010.pdf

Dangerousness assessment:

Dr. Jacquelyn Campbell, a leading domestic violence researcher who created the original Dangerous Assessment tool, has identified the following risk factors in assessing the level of danger presented by an abuser:

- Access to/ownership of guns
- Use of weapons in prior abusive incidents
- Threats with weapons
- Serious injury in prior abusive incidents
- Threats of suicide or murder
- Drug or alcohol abuse
- Forced sex of female partner
- Obsessiveness/extreme jealousy/extreme dominance
- End of the relationship
- Stalking
- Escalation of violence
- Choking and strangling in the past

It is important to remember that no instrument, no matter how thorough, should take the place of counselors and advocates working with survivors to individually identify their level of danger and decide the most appropriate course of action. Ultimately, the abused woman (or man) is the best judge of the danger she/he is in and needs to be encouraged to listen to her/his instincts.

To access Dr. Campbell's Danger Assessment Tool, go to www.dangerassessment.org/uploads/pdf/DAEnglish2010.pdf

Safety precautions related to technology:

- Use a public computer at the library, a friend's computer or your computer at work to prevent your abuser from tracking your online activity. Your abuser can go through your history and can also monitor your activity through spyware. Clear your browsing history frequently.

- Try to change your email password to something no one will be able to guess or create a new account of which the abuser is unaware.

- Consider getting a phone not provided or paid for by your abuser. Otherwise, the abuser can track calls using your phone bill. In addition, the abuser can regularly scroll through the phone and see who has called and texted you, and may have installed software on your phone to enable monitoring from another phone or computer. If your phone has an optional GPS location service, keep it turned off.

- Change your phone password frequently, to limit access.

- Check your car, both inside and out for any suspicious objects. It is possible that your abuser may have placed a GPS Tracking device in your car.

- Contact an advocate in a local domestic violence program to help you create a technology safety plan and make changes to your technology. nnedv.org/downloads/ SafetyNet/OVW/NNEDV_HighTechStalking_ Tipsheet_2010.pdf and www.movanet.org

Getting an ex-parte temporary restraining order:

A restraining order is a court order that can be useful for keeping an abuser from having any contact with you, the survivor. You can apply for a restraining order (also called a 209A) by going to a courthouse and completing the forms. It is free and you do not need identification. When you have completed the forms, the clerk will take the order to the judge and you will find out that day whether you are granted a temporary ex-parte order. (Ex-parte means that only one party provided evidence, in this case, you.) When the court is closed, you may obtain an emergency ex-parte restraining order by going to your local police station.

In order to be granted the ex-parte temporary order, you must demonstrate to the court that the defendant (abuser) hurt or tried to physically hurt you, made you afraid of imminent physical harm, and/or forced you to engage in sexual relations against your will. The judge is looking for recent acts of violence that include: physical assault, threats, interfering with freedom (i.e. blocking entry to a doorway, taking a phone out of your hand when trying to make a call, taking car keys), destruction of property, unauthorized entry (breaking into your home, car, work, or school), sexual assault, harassment (repeated communication at inconvenient hours, unwanted gifts, insults, phone calls), and stalking (a pattern of two or more unwanted contacts).

The temporary ex-parte order will remain in effect from the time the defendant is served until the next court hearing. The next court hearing, which will determine if the order is extended, is generally scheduled within 10 business days. Your local crisis center can be very helpful in drafting the affidavit (declaration of what happened), including what information to include.

They may also have resources for getting a pro bono attorney and/or an advocate to accompany you to the 10-day extension hearing.

If you have children, you will need to complete additional paperwork about your children, including if you want the judge to grant you custody of your children and if you want the judge to order the defendant to pay child support. The judge can grant you custody of your children at the ex-parte hearing, but cannot award you child support at the ex-parte hearing. However, the judge can award you child support at the 10-day extension hearing and it is a much simpler process to request child support when you first complete the forms for a restraining order.

Additional resources related to restraining orders include:

- Mass Legal Help for forms available in English and Spanish: www.masslegalhelp.org/domestic-violence/abuse-prevention-orders

- The Battered Women's Justice Project (bwjp.org) has a free online guide with information about protection orders called *Increasing Your Safety: Full Faith and Credit for Protection Orders*

- Women's Bar Association Family Law Project for Battered Women www.womensbar.org/

- National District Attorneys Association: www.ndaa.org/pdf/strangulation_statutory_compilation_11_7_2014.pdf

Resources for friends and family members of survivors:

The impact of domestic violence ripples beyond just the survivor and affects family, friends, and the surrounding community. Resources for families include:

How to Help a Loved One: Do's and Don'ts: www.abuseintervention.org/sandbox77/wp-content/uploads/2012/03/How-to-Help-a-Loved-One.pdf

FAQ Domestic Violence: www.thefamilytree.org/en/domestic-violence-services/156#listitem557-1959

For Families, Friends, and Neighbors: www.dvrcv.org.au/help-advice/guide-for-families-friends-and-neighbours

About domestic violence:

For why women stay in abusive relationships, go to:

- National Network to End Violence: nnedv.org/resources/stats/faqaboutdv

- Sarah M. Buell's *50 Obstacles to Leaving:* www.sdcedsv.org/media/sdcedsvfactor360com/uploads/Articles/50Obstacles.pdf

To learn more about risk factors contributing to Intimate Partner Violence, see the Center for Disease Control and Prevention (CDC): www.cdc.gov/violenceprevention/intimatepartnerviolence/riskprotectivefactors.html

For information on animal abuse and family violence, see the following organizations:

- RedRover: www.redrover.org
- Allie Phillips: www.alliephillips.com/saf-tprogram
- National Link Coalition: www.nationallinkcoalition.org

The National Network to End Domestic Violence presents Biderman's Chart of Coercion, a tool that explains the methods used to break down and brainwash prisoners of war. Batterers use these same techniques to break the will of their victims: www.nnedv.org/images/Transitional_Housing/Trauma_Informed_Services_Handout.pdf

The Power and Control Wheel, created by The Domestic Violence Intervention Project, is a diagram that demonstrates the typical patterns of abusive and violent behaviors used by an abuser to establish and maintain control: www.theduluthmodel.org/pdf/powerandcontrol.pdf

Self-care and grounding techniques:

- Anxiety grounding techniques: www.healthyplace.com/blogs/treatinganxiety/2010/09/top-21-anxiety-grounding-techniques

- Grounding techniques: www.get.gg/flashbacks.htm

- Mindful meditation app: www.calm.com

- Self-compassion: www.selfcompassion.org

Additional reading on domestic violence:

- *Why Does He Do That?* by Lundy Bancroft

- *The Emotionally Abusive Marriage,* by Leslie Vernick

- *The Verbally Abusive Relationship,* by Patricia Evans

- *Trauma and Recovery,* by Judith Herman

- *When Love Hurts,* by Jill Corey and Karen McAndless-Davis

- *The Power to Break Free,* by Anisha Durve

- *Invisible Chains: Overcoming Coercive Control in Your Intimate Relationship*, by Lisa Aronson Fontes, PhD

- *Listening to Battered Women: A Survivor-Centered Approach to Advocacy, Mental Health, and Justice,* by Lisa Goodman, PhD

Citations By Chapter

Introduction

Department of Justice. (2015). Domestic Violence. *Office on Violence Against Women*. Retrieved from www.justice.gov/ovw/domestic-violence

Durve, A. (2012). Appendix 1 statistics on domestic violence. In *The power to break free: Surviving domestic violence: With a special reference to abuse in Indian marriages* (pp. 381). Cleveland, OH: Power Press LLC.

Enayati, A. (2012). The importance of belonging. *CNN Health*. Retrieved from www.cnn.com/2012/06/01/health/enayati-importance-of-belonging/index.html

Herman, J. (1992). Disconnection. In *Trauma and recovery: The aftermath of violence from domestic abuse to political terror* (pp. 51). New York, NY: Basic Books.

National Network to End Domestic Violence. (2014). Domestic and sexual violence fact sheet. Retrieved from nnedv.org/downloads/Policy/AD14/AD14_DVSA_Factsheet.pdf

Walton, G. M., Cohen, G. L., Cwir, D., & Spencer, S. J. (2012). Mere belonging: Power of social connections. *Journal of Personality and Social Psychology, 102*(3), 513-532.

PART ONE
Get Real: Acknowledging What's True

The Women Of The Second Step Narrative Healing Group

2015 Trafficking in Persons Report (Rep.). (n.d.). Retrieved from www.state.gov/documents/organization/243562.pdf

Durve, A. (2012). The psychology of abuse. In *The power to break free: Surviving domestic violence: With a special reference to abuse in Indian marriages* (pp. 75 & 77). Cleveland, OH: Power Press LLC.

Human Trafficking. (2012, June 13). Retrieved May, 2016, from www.nij.gov/topics/crime/human-trafficking/pages/welcome.aspx

What You Should Know About Domestic Violence. (2016). Retrieved from www.dcadv.org/what-you-should-know-about-domestic-violence

First Encounters With Love

About the CDC-Kaiser ACE Study. (2016, March 08). Retrieved May 2016, from www.cdc.gov/violenceprevention/acestudy/about.html

Nakazawa, D. (2015, August 7). 7 Ways Childhood Adversity Can Change Your Brain. Retrieved May 2016, from www.psychologytoday.com/blog/the-last-best-cure/201508/7-ways-childhood adversity-changes-your-brain

PTSD: National Center for PTSD. (2015, August 13). Retrieved May 2016, from www.ptsd.va.gov/public/PTSD-overview/basics/what-is-ptsd.asp

What is Domestic Violence? (n.d.). Retrieved May 2016, from www.ncadv.org/need-help/what-is-domestic-violence

False First Impressions

Aronson Fontes, L. (2015). Controlling behaviors. In *Invisible chains: Overcoming coercive control in your intimate relationships* (pp. 52). New York, NY: Guilford Press.

Bancroft, L. (2002). How abuse begins. In *Why does he do that: Inside the minds of angry and controlling men* (pp. 121-122). New York, NY: Penguin Putnam Inc.

Bancroft, L., & Silverman, J. G. (2002). The batterer as parent: Addressing the impact of domestic violence on family dynamics. Thousand Oaks, CA: Sage Publications.

Domestic Violence and Pregnancy. (2016). Retrieved May 2016, from www.ucsfhealth.org/education/domestic_violence_and_pregnancy/

Martin, D. (1976). The batterer: What makes him a brute? In *Battered wives* (p. 61). San Francisco, CA: Glide Publications.

WHO Multi-country Study on Women's Health and Domestic Violence against Women. (2005). Retrieved from www.who.int/gender/violence/who_multicountry_study/summary_report/summary_report_English2.pdf

It's Complicated

Campbell, J. C., Glass, N., Sharps, P. W., Laughon, K., & Bloom, T. (2007). Intimate Partner Homicide: Review and Implications of Research and Policy. *Trauma, Violence, & Abuse*, 8(3), 246-269.

Campbell, J., Webster, D., Koziol-McLean, J., & McFarlane, J. (2003). Risk Factors for Intimate Partner Femecide. *American Journal of Public Health*. 10, 89-97.

Domestic Violence: Explore the Issue. (2003). Retrieved May 2016, from www1.umn.edu/humanrts/svaw/domestic/link/alcohol.htm

Goodman, L. A. & Epstein, D. (2008). The need for continued reform: The broad scope and deep impact of intimate partner violence. In *Listening to battered women: A survivor-centered approach to advocacy, mental health, and justice* (pp. 9). Washington D.C.: American Psychological Association.

Renick, R. (2012). Biderman's chart of coercion [Chart]. In *National Network to End Domestic Violence*. Retrieved from nnedv.org/images/Transitional_Housing/Trauma_Informed_Services_Handout.pdf

PART TWO
Get Help: Finding The Strength To Reach Out

Thinking About Leaving

Bancroft, L. (2002). The abusive man and breaking up. In *Why does he do that: Inside the minds of angry and controlling men* (pp.213). New York, NY: Penguin Group.

Intimate Partner Violence: Consequences. (2015, March 03). Retrieved May 2016, from www.cdc.gov/ViolencePrevention/intimatepartnerviolence/consequences.html

National Coalition Against Domestic Violence. (2015). *Pets and Domestic Violence* [Brochure]. Retrieved from www.hope-eci.org/_documents/petsanddv.pdf

Path to Safety. (2015). Retrieved May 2016, from www.thehotline.org/help/path-to-safety

Technology Abuse: Experiences of Survivors and Victim Service Agencies. (2014, April 29). Retrieved from nnedv.org/news/4272-new-survey-technology-abuse-experiences-of-survivors-and-victim-service-agencie.html

Schwartz, A. (2012, March 13). Family Boundaries and the Parentified Child [Web log post]. Retrieved from www.mentalhelp.net/blogs/family-boundaries-and-the-parentified-child/

Shout It From The Mountaintops

Aronson Fontes, L. (2015). Introduction to coercive control. In *Invisible chains: Overcoming coercive control in your intimate relationships* (pp. 5). New York, NY: Guilford Press.

Durve, A. (2012). The Indian victim & karma. In *The power to break free: Surviving domestic violence: With a special reference to abuse in Indian marriages* (pp.373). Cleveland, OH: Power Press LLC.

It Ain't Over Yet

Campbell, J. C., Glass, N., Sharps, P. W., Laughon, K., & Bloom, T. (2007). Intimate Partner Homicide: Review and Implications of Research and Policy. *Trauma, Violence, & Abuse,* 8(3), 246-269.

Caring For Your Cubs

Groves, B. M., LICSW. (2012). *The Impact of Domestic Violence on Children: What Research Tells Us and Why it is Relevant.*

Presentation. Retrieved from www.cga.ct.gov/coc/pdfs/domestic_violence/mcalister-groves_dv_ppt.pdf

The National Child Traumatic Stress Network. (2014). *Children and Domestic Violence Listening and Talking to Your Child About Domestic Violence* [Factsheet]. Retrieved from www.nctsn.org/sites/default/files/assets/pdfs/childrenanddv_factsheet_4.pdf

Self Help - Useful Articles. (2016). Retrieved May 2016, from www.ipfw.edu/affiliates/assistance/selfhelp/relationship-settingboundaries.html

A Message To Caregivers And Loved Ones

Domestic Abuse Intervention Services. (2012). [Brochure]. Retrieved from: www.abuseintervention.org/sandbox77/wp-content/uploads/2012/03/How-to-Help-a-Loved-One.pdf

Violence Against Women. (2015, September 4). Retrieved May 2016, from www.womenshealth.gov/violence-against-women/get-help-for-violence/how-to-help-a-friend-who-is-being-abused.html

Yau, R. (2012, December 7). 16 Safe and Creative Ways for Bystanders to Become Upstanders in Stopping Violence Against Women. Retrieved May 2016, from 16days.thepixelproject.net/16-safe-and-creative-ways-for-bystanders-to-become-upstanders-in-stopping-violence-against-women/

PART THREE
Get Healed: Moving From Surviving To Thriving

An Imperfect System

About the Domestic Violence High Risk Team (DVHRT) Model. (2016). Retrieved May 2016, from www.dvhrt.org/ about Thurman v. City of Torrington (United States District Court October 23, 1984) (Berkman Center for Internet & Society at Harvard University, Dist. file).

There's Nothing Broken That Can't Be Fixed

Lafata, L. (2001). Five practices for a sustainable life. [Handout].

Navigating New Relationships

History of Battered Women's Movement. (1999, September). Retrieved May 2016, from www.icadvinc.org/what-is-domestic-violence/history-of-battered-womens-movement/

Where We Are Now

Bremner, D. J., M.D. (2000, March). The Invisible Epidemic: Post-Traumatic Stress Disorder, Memory and the Brain. Retrieved May 2016, from www.pandys.org/articles/invisibleepidemic. html

Neff, K. (2015). Definition and Three Elements of Self-Compassion. Retrieved May 2016, from self-compassion.org/ the-three-elements-of-self-compassion-2/

About The Facilitators And Editor

Carole Thompson is Director of Community Programs at The Second Step, where she has served since 1999. She holds an MS in Counseling Psychology, with a focus on College Student Development, from Northeastern University, a Certificate in Trauma Stress Studies from HRI (the Trauma Center), and has completed the life coach curriculum through The Coaches Training Institute. Prior to her work in the field of domestic violence, she served as Associate Dean for Student Life at Pine Manor College.

Sherry Katz is an organizational consultant and certified life coach. She has a 30-year career working with corporations on team building, communication, and change management. Seven years ago she began volunteering at The Second Step, co-leading two groups, mentoring survivors, and organizing their annual "Day of Beauty" event. Sherry has an MEd in Counseling Psychology and an MS in Organizational Development.

Sharon Johnson is a former president of The Second Step board of directors. She likes to think that while she makes a living as a corporate writer, she makes a life as a ghostwriter. It has been a pleasure and a privilege to work with the gutsy, funny, resilient, courageous and determined women of The Second Step Narrative Healing Group.

About The Second Step

The Second Step (TSS) fosters the safety, stability, and well-being of survivors of domestic violence. Our residential and community-based programs build on the strengths, needs, and values of the individuals and families we serve. In partnership with survivors and in collaboration with the community, we lay a foundation for a future free from abuse and full of possibility.

Founded in 1992, The Second Step has partnered with thousands of survivors to address the aftermath of abuse and build brighter futures for themselves and their children. TSS also works to address the root causes of domestic violence and end it in our time. The need is urgent, and it is not enough just to respond. We must work to prevent and uproot the sources of gender-based and domestic violence in order to break a cycle that can span generations.

TSS's approach to this is unique. Our work relies on a close, supportive, long-term relationship between survivors and their advocates. Core to our operating philosophy and our theory of change is the belief that:

> (1) survivor empowerment has profound social, emotional, and material consequences;

> (2) this empowerment is something we as an agency and as individual advocates have the power to develop in alliance with the survivor;

> (3) this alliance is driven by a commitment to the survivor's own individual needs.

To learn more about The Second Step, go to www.thesecondstep.org.

In Gratitude

We thank the following people, who have done so much to help us make this book a reality:

Our Angel Donor, who believed in us from the beginning, and provided the financial support to make this book a reality.

Sarah Perry, Executive Director of The Second Step, for championing our multi-year book-writing endeavor.

Keith Leon and the publishing team at Leon Smith Publishing, for their sage advice, unflagging patience, and deep commitment to the issues of domestic violence.

Jenevieve Maerker, Esq. and her team at Foley Hoag LLP for their generosity, stellar legal guidance, and technical support.

Isabelle Thacker, Director of Steps to Justice at The Second Step, for her support and thoughtful recommendations throughout the process.

Sophie Massey, for her superb research and writing contributions.

Domenica Rizza, whose academic slant helped guide our research on resources.

Lora Brody, for her photography and creativity.

Mark Farber and Stephen Thompson, for their attention to detail in the final editing process.

Margaret Coughlin and Beryl Loeb, for their public relations wisdom and advice.

Mayapriya Long, our book cover designer, for her creativity and willingness to go beyond.

Sabrina Fiaz, for her knowledge and attention to detail in editing citations.

Heidi Bluming, a Second Step intern, for her work leading group exercises.

Claudia Olds Goldie, for her insight, creativity and ongoing support.

Christ the King Church, Newton, for so generously sponsoring our book launch party.

Most importantly, to Amber, a survivor who made guest appearances in our book and who shared her deep wisdom and life experiences with us.

# # #

Made in the USA
Middletown, DE
28 October 2016